The Resurrection
of Jesus Christ
in New Testament Theology

Books by John Frederick Jansen

PUBLISHED BY THE WESTMINSTER PRESS

*The Resurrection of Jesus Christ
in New Testament Theology*

*Guests of God:
Meditations for the Lord's Supper*

The Meaning of Baptism: Meditations

The Resurrection
of Jesus Christ
in New Testament Theology

John Frederick Jansen

The Westminster Press
Philadelphia

First edition

Published by The Westminster Press ®
Philadelphia, Pennsylvania

PRINTED IN THE UNITED STATES OF AMERICA

9 8 7 6 5 4 3 2 1

Library of Congress Cataloging in Publication Data

Jansen, John Frederick.
　The resurrection of Jesus Christ in New Testament theology.

　Includes bibliographical references and index.
　1. Jesus Christ—Resurrection. 2. Bible.
N.T.—Criticism, interpretation, etc. I. Title.
BT481.J32　　232′.5　　80–231
ISBN 0–664–24309–6

To our sons
John, Tyler, Mark, David, Andy
that they may be
"sons of the resurrection" (Lk. 20:36)

O world invisible, we view thee,
O world intangible, we touch thee,
O world unknowable, we know thee,
Inapprehensible, we clutch thee!

. . . .

The angels keep their ancient places;—
Turn but a stone and start a wing!
'Tis ye, 'tis your estrangèd faces,
That miss the many-splendoured thing.

—Francis Thompson, "In No Strange Land"

Contents

Preface

Recent years have witnessed a great number of books and articles on the resurrection of Jesus Christ. They range from specialized monographs of New Testament research and significant volumes in systematic theology to the more popular volumes addressed to the general reader. Almost every possible point of view has found expression.

The present volume is not an exegetical contribution to New Testament research but an attempt to describe Easter's significance in the New Testament as a whole—to see Easter's meaning as a unifying focus in the rich diversity of New Testament thought and life. It represents a refinement and development of an essay, "The Resurrection of Jesus Christ in New Testament Theology," that appeared in the faculty edition of the *Austin Seminary Bulletin* of September 1973. That essay was a programmatic sketch reached after a half year's sabbatical study at the University of Leiden in 1971. The present volume was made possible through a half year of sabbatical study at the University of Cambridge in 1978.

Biblical theology is not only the concern of specialists. It is done in and for the church. Accordingly, this volume seeks to interpret the shape of the New Testament's Easter message for those most involved in the worship and life of the church: pastors and laypersons. It has grown out of church seminars, both clergy and lay, as well as out of courses and projects with seminary students. The accompanying notes indicate in some bibliographical detail the basis for the exposition.

It is not possible to express my debt to all those whose interest, insight, and critique have helped me in the preparation and completion of this work. Among friends in Cambridge, Professor C. F. D. Moule graciously read my earlier essay and made helpful suggestions. In Austin, colleagues and students have helped me in countless ways. The final writing has benefited from helpful suggestions by John E. Alsup, Robert M. Shelton, and Merwyn Johnson. Special thanks go to Louise Wilson and Bobbi Sanders, who commented on an earlier draft as lay theologians. Joseph R. Cooper read the earlier draft from the perspective of a pastor. As always, my wife has helped me with her comments on the final draft—not to speak of her patience during the whole process. Of course, I am responsible for the book's shortcomings.

J.F.J.

I

Approaching the Message of the Resurrection

The resurrection of Jesus Christ is the starting point for the Christian church and for the writing of the New Testament. The unity of New Testament faith lies in its confession that the crucified Jesus is the Son of God in power and the Lord of life through his resurrection from the dead. Explicit references to his resurrection are found in all of the New Testament documents except 2 Thessalonians, Titus, Philemon, 2 Peter, 3 John, and Jude. Implicit testimony narrows the exception to 3 John, which is wholly devoted to a particular ecclesiastical problem. While the other documents just mentioned do not explicitly speak of the resurrection, they bear witness to the living Lord by linking the grace of the Lord Jesus to the love of God the Father and by affirming that the future is entrusted to him as the Lord of glory who will come from heaven. The centrality of the resurrection for faith does not need demonstration.[1]

But what does the resurrection of Jesus Christ mean? How are we to understand its significance for faith? To read the extensive literature on the resurrection discloses a wide diversity of interpretation.

DIVERSE EXPRESSIONS OF EASTER FAITH

In 1967, Berthold Klappert[2] introduced a volume of readings from recent Easter discussions by suggesting that in the

New Testament one can find at least five principal concerns or "orientation points" of Easter faith. One is historical concern for the reality of the resurrection: What happened? What can we know? A second is concern for the saving significance of the resurrection: How are we justified? How is the resurrection the ground of our redemption? A third is concern for the eschatological significance of the resurrection: What may we hope for? A fourth is concern for the message of the church: What is our message? To what are we sent? A fifth is concern for the resurrection as the ground of personal faith: How do we understand ourselves? How is our own coming to faith related to the Easter confession? Klappert cautioned against elevating any of these five "orientation points" as a sufficient interpretation of Easter. His volume of readings shows that all too often this is precisely what has happened in the various interpretations of Easter faith.

More recently Gerald O'Collins, in a little volume entitled *What Are They Saying About the Resurrection?*[3] has adapted these five orientation points and sought to illustrate them as "models of the resurrection," adding a sixth model, "The Resurrection as Revelation." He begins his survey of recent discussions with the words: "Despite all their debates and polemic, many scholars have not in fact been simply on a collision course with each other. They have specialized in one or other model in reflecting on the many-faceted mystery which is the Lord's rising from the dead."[4] However, when one model or orientation point is seen as sufficient interpretation to the exclusion of others, irreconcilable positions do result. For example, if the only Easter "history" is my own coming to faith in the saving significance of the cross, if Christ is present in my experience without first having had his own Easter history, something central has been lost in the New Testament message.[5] Here we shall not trace the various directions of the recent debates, for this has been done in a number of recent volumes.[6] It is sufficient to note that the New Testament itself portrays the resurrection of Jesus as a "many-splendoured thing," so that its united witness to the centrality of Easter is not a uniform witness but one that embraces a rich diversity of expression.

DIVERSITY OF FORM

The diversity of the New Testament is evident, of course, in the variety of its literary forms—gospel, acts, epistles, apocalypse—as well as in the various literary genres within these books (hymn, creed, catechetical instruction, etc.). Literary diversity is manifest in the various forms in which the Easter faith finds expression. While we often begin with the Gospel narratives of the empty tomb and appearances, we need to remember that there are many formulas of confession embedded in the various New Testament books.[7] For example:

The gospel concerning his Son,
who was descended from David according to the flesh and
designated Son of God in power according to the Spirit
    of holiness by his resurrection from the dead,
Jesus Christ our Lord. (Rom. 1:3–4)

(That is, the word of faith which we preach);
because, if you confess with your lips that
    Jesus is Lord
and believe in your heart
    that God raised him from the dead,
you will be saved. (Rom. 10:8–9)

For I delivered to you as of first importance what I
    also received,
that Christ died for our sins in accordance with the
    scriptures,
that he was buried,
that he was raised on the third day in accordance with
    the scriptures,
and that he appeared to Cephas, then to the twelve.
(1 Cor. 15:3–5)

In addition to such confessions of faith there are also the more antithetic formulas in the speeches of Acts that constitute a call to repentance:

> This Jesus, delivered up according to the definite plan and foreknowledge of God, you crucified and killed by the hands of lawless men. But God raised him up, having loosed the pangs of death, because it was not possible for him to be held by it. (Acts 2:23–24)

> But you denied the Holy and Righteous One . . . and killed the Author of life, whom God raised from the dead. (Acts 3:14–15)

> The God of our fathers raised Jesus whom you killed by hanging him on a tree. God exalted him at his right hand as Leader and Savior, to give repentance to Israel and forgiveness of sins. (Acts 5:30–31)

Some of these early summaries point backward to the earthly life and work of Jesus (e.g., Acts 2:22ff.; 10:36ff.); others point forward to his future role in judgment (e.g., Acts 17:31; 1 Thess. 1:9–10).

DIVERSITY OF VOCABULARY

A wider diversity marks the vocabulary.[8] As some of the early confessions are more hymnic than sermonic or apologetic, so is the language different. Often we meet a vocabulary and imagery of "exaltation" rather than a vocabulary and imagery of "resurrection." For example:

> Who, though he was in the form of God,
> did not count equality with God
> a thing to be grasped,
>
> but emptied himself,
> taking the form of a servant,
> being born in the likeness of men.
>
> And being found in human form
> he humbled himself

and became obedient unto death,
  even death on a cross.

Therefore God has highly exalted him
and bestowed on him the name which is
above every name,

that at the name of Jesus
every knee should bow,
in heaven and on earth and under the earth,

and every tongue confess that
Jesus Christ is Lord,
to the glory of God the Father. (Phil. 2:6–11)

He is the head of the body, the church;
he is the beginning, the first-born from the dead,
that in everything he might be pre-eminent. (Col. 1:18)

He who descended is he who also ascended
far above all the heavens,
that he might fill all things. (Eph. 4:10)

He was manifested in the flesh,
vindicated in the Spirit,
seen by angels,
preached among the nations,
believed on in the world,
taken up in glory. (1 Tim. 3:16)

Sometimes a New Testament writer employs both the vocabulary of resurrection and that of exaltation, sometimes one or the other. Sometimes no distinction is drawn between resurrection and exaltation; sometimes the latter appears to follow the former. Only Luke makes a clear temporal distinction by placing the ascension forty days after the resurrection.

DIVERSITY IN THE NARRATIVES

Anyone who has compared the Easter narratives of the four Gospels is aware that they too exhibit diversity. While the narrative of the empty tomb is common to all four Gospels, even this witness is not uniform. Who went to the tomb? All four Gospels mention Mary Magdalene, but the Synoptic Gospels vary in the names of the other women, while Luke and John mention disciples as well.[9] Mark and Luke say that the women came to anoint the body of Jesus, but Matthew says that the tomb was sealed and guarded, while John says that Joseph of Arimathea and Nicodemus had already anointed the body at burial.

Where and when and how many times did the risen Christ appear to his followers? In Matthew and John there is an appearance at the tomb to the women or to Mary alone. Matthew has one appearance to the eleven, while Luke has an appearance on the road to Emmaus as well as an appearance to the gathered disciples, and a reference to an appearance to Peter. In his second volume, The Acts, Luke adds other appearances. John has two appearances to disciples, and the epilogue to his Gospel describes a further meeting. The Lord's appearances occur in Galilee (implied in Mark, explicit in Matthew and in John 21, whereas in Luke and in John 20 the appearances are in Jerusalem and its vicinity. Other questions are raised by the list of appearances cited in 1 Cor. 15:5–8, for these cannot be harmonized with the Gospel narratives.[10] Indeed, nowhere is the diversity of the New Testament seen more clearly than in its varied witness to the resurrection of Jesus.

If the Easter traditions present diversity, this diversity bears its own witness to the depths of Easter's meaning, as we shall see.

UNITY IN DIVERSITY: "IN ACCORDANCE WITH THE SCRIPTURES"

The early Easter creed in 1 Corinthians 15 affirms that Christ died and was raised "in accordance with the scriptures."[11] Since the Scriptures of the Old Testament are not uniform in their witness to a resurrection of the dead, how are we to understand that Christ was raised "in accordance with the scriptures"?

We can point, of course, to particular Old Testament texts that have a prominent place in the proclamation of the early church. Such texts include the royal psalms of enthronement such as Ps. 2 (e.g., Acts 13:33, "This he has fulfilled to us their children by raising Jesus; as also it is written in the second psalm, 'Thou art my Son, today I have begotten thee' "), and Ps. 110 (e.g., Acts 2:34, "For David did not ascend into the heavens; but he himself says, 'The Lord said to my Lord, Sit at my right hand' "). With its imagery of "at the right hand," it is not surprising that this psalm should be prominent in the New Testament witness to the risen and exalted Christ. Luke adds Ps. 16:10 in the speeches of Acts 2 and 13 (e.g., Acts 2:27, "nor let thy Holy One see corruption").

In their own setting these psalms did not envision a messiah's resurrection, but the New Testament witnesses come to such texts through their faith that "all the promises of God find their Yes in him" (2 Cor. 1:20). Easter sent the early church back to its Scriptures to understand and to proclaim the resurrection of Jesus.

The same holds true for those Old Testament texts which represent an emerging apocalyptic tradition of a final resurrection of the dead (e.g., Isa. 26:19; Daniel 7; 12), a tradition that comes to fuller expression in the intertestamental literature. The doctrine of a final resurrection of the dead had become part of Pharisaic belief in the time of Jesus. However, because the doctrine was not taught in the Torah (the Pentateuch), it was still sharply contested by the Sadducees in the time of Jesus (cf. Mk. 12:18ff. and its parallels; Acts 4:1–2; etc.). While Jn. 11:24 suggests that Martha shared this hope ("I know that he [Lazarus] will rise again in the resurrection at the last day"), there is also evidence that even disciples were unsure, "questioning what the rising from the dead meant" (Mk. 9:10).

In any case, the apocalyptic tradition included a resurrection of the dead at the end of time; it did not envision the resurrection of one man in the middle of time. At most, we have flickering lights in the Old Testament and in the later tradition of Judaism.

To be sure, there is some indication of belief in an individual resurrection (better, an ascension or assumption) of particular figures such as Enoch and Elijah. In recent investigation Klaus Berger[12] has drawn attention to the anxiety of Herod about John the Baptist. "King Herod heard of it; for Jesus' name had become known. Some said, 'John the baptizer has been raised from the dead; that is why these powers are at work in him.' But others said, 'It is Elijah.' And others said, 'It is a prophet, like one of the prophets of old.' But when Herod heard of it he said, 'John, whom I beheaded, has been raised' " (Mk. 6:14–16 and parallels in Mt. 14:1ff. and Lk. 9:7ff.). Similarly, when Jesus asked his disciples who people said he was, they answered, "John the Baptist; and others say, Elijah; and others one of the prophets" (Mk. 8:28; cf. Lk. 9:19; Mt. 16:14 adds "Jeremiah or one of the prophets"). Berger notes that in 2 Macc. 15:13–16, Judas Maccabeus encouraged his followers by telling them of a dream in which a man of majesty and authority "who loves the brethren and prays much for the people and the holy city, Jeremiah, the prophet of God" had given him a golden sword. Similarly, in the vision of the two witnesses in Revelation 11, New Testament faith portrays the resurrection and vindication of Jesus as the eschatological prophet of God. Be that as it may, these traditions of an "exalted" prophet do not prepare us for the "bodily" resurrection of Jesus in the Easter narratives. New Testament Christology certainly includes in the titles of Jesus "the prophet" of the end time (cf. the use of Deut. 18:15 in Acts 3:22 and 7:37), but Jesus is more than "the prophet"; he is the Son of God, Messiah, and Lord.

All this makes clear that the disciples did not simply come to Easter faith through the apocalyptic tradition, however much they may have appropriated this tradition to illumine and to describe the Easter faith. Here we may think of Acts 4:2, where Sadducees are annoyed because the disciples were proclaiming "in Jesus the resurrection from the dead" (NEB: "proclaiming the resurrection from the dead—the resurrection of Jesus"). In Acts, Paul sees the hope of the future guaranteed in the proleptic resurrection of Jesus because "by being the first to rise from the dead, he would proclaim light both to the people and to the Gentiles" (Acts 26:23). Here the resurrection of Jesus becomes the validation of Pharisaic hope (Acts 26:5–7; NEB: "I lived as a Pharisee. And it is for a hope kindled by God's promise to our forefathers that I stand in the dock today . . . and for this very hope I am impeached").

Withal, the phrase "in accordance with the scriptures" takes us beyond some isolated texts often cited in the New Testament, and beyond a particular apocalyptic tradition. According to Luke 24:27 and 44, the risen Lord, beginning with Moses and all the prophets, "interpreted to them in all the scriptures the things concerning himself."

What does this suggest about early Christian use of the Old Testament? Too often New Testament theology has tended to narrow its focus by looking to the Old Testament only as a background for the New. If New Testament theology is truly biblical theology, it must take more seriously the whole of Scripture as canon. If, as the New Testament affirms, the God and Father of Jesus is the God of Israel, we cannot simply isolate certain Old Testament texts and traditions. We must ask if there is not a more inclusive way of understanding the claim that Christ was raised according to the Scriptures. The earliest church did not turn to the "Old Testament" as background material for its faith. After all, the Old Testament was the Bible, the only Bible, for the earliest church.

This is the plea of Peter Stuhlmacher,[13] who sees in the Easter faith the pivotal expression of a biblical theology which affirms that the God of Israel is the God of righteousness who vindicates his righteousness. Jesus is the "Righteous One" (Acts 3:14). In the resurrection and vindication of Jesus the earliest church saw the completion and goal of Israel's faith in God. Jesus was understood and misunderstood by disciples and opponents in the framework of Israelite conceptions of salvation. Long before and even quite apart from a later apocalyptic tradition, Israel's faith knew that God is the Lord of life and death. Hannah's song could exult that "the Lord kills and brings to life; he brings down to Sheol and raises up" (1 Sam. 2:6).[14] It is this biblical faith that finds its ultimate expression in the Easter faith of the New Testament church.

This has implications for the way in which we do biblical theology. For example, is it really sufficient or decisive to look for one particular Old Testament text that may lie behind the early creed's assertion "that he was raised on the third day in accordance with the scriptures" (1 Cor. 15:4)? As we shall see, most scholars have sought this text in Hos. 6:2 ("After two days he will revive us; on the third day he will raise us up, that we may live before him"), assuming that this is the key text which must have been interpreted Christologically by the early church.[15] However, quite apart from the fact that this text is never cited in the New Testament, the early creed speaks of "scriptures," not "scripture." Is it sufficient to find one particular text that mentions "the third day"?[16] Is there not a more inclusive approach (as in Lk. 24:27, 44ff.) in which the whole of God's story with his people is seen fulfilled in the resurrection of Jesus?

A good example of the kind of biblical theology to which Stuhlmacher invites us can be seen in the Lukan speech of Paul in Acts 13:17ff. In that speech we meet not only citations of such characteristic Old Testament texts as Ps. 2 and

16; we meet also a larger rehearsal of Israel's story in which the resurrection of Jesus is seen as the focus and fulfillment of this whole story.

> Men of Israel, and you that fear God, listen. The God of this people Israel chose our fathers and made the people great during their stay in the land of Egypt, and with uplifted arm he led them out of it. . . . He gave them their land. . . . He gave them judges. . . . God gave them Saul the son of Kish. . . . He raised up *(ēgeiren)* David to be their king. . . . Of this man's posterity God has brought to Israel a Savior, Jesus, as he promised. . . . Though they could charge him with nothing deserving death, yet they asked Pilate to have him killed. And when they had fulfilled all that was written of him, they took him down from the tree, and laid him in a tomb. But God raised *(ēgeiren)* him from the dead; and for many days he appeared to those who came up with him from Galilee to Jerusalem, who are now his witnesses to the people. And we bring you the good news that what God promised to the fathers, this he has fulfilled to us their children by raising *(anastēsas)* Jesus; as also it is written in the second psalm."

This has further implications. When New Testament studies have separated the Easter faith of the early church from the Old Testament except for noting some isolated texts or calling attention to an apocalyptic background of thought, they have often sought analogies to the Easter faith in the general religious environment of early Christianity, whether in the dying and rising deities of the mystery religions or in the apotheosis and deification of a "divine man" like Romulus or Apollonius.[17] However, if New Testament faith sees Jesus as the revelation of the God of Israel, it is much more likely that an Old Testament literary genre of revelatory disclosure will provide analogies to the manner in which the risen Jesus reveals himself to his followers as the Son of God. That is to say, the tradition behind our Gospel narratives of the Easter Christ's appearances is analogous to some of the Old Testament theophanies in which the divine presence is portrayed as becoming visible and audible in tangible form.[18]

A good example is found in Genesis 18,[19] where the Lord "appeared" to Abraham at Mamre in visible human form. As in the Easter narratives, such Old Testament theophanies not only have the characteristic verb "appeared," but portray the divine presence with tangible and anthropomorphic features of hospitality and table fellowship. Frequently, too, we meet the words "Fear not" to assuage the confusion and bewilderment of those encountered by the divine presence. The Easter appearances may not be exact parallels to such Old Testament theophanies, but they do resemble them in calling attention to "the elusive presence."[20]

This is not to suggest that Easter faith is derived from a reading of the Old Testament any more than that God's promised redemption of exiles from Babylon was simply a recollection or repetition of the exodus redemption. To those exiles the prophetic word heard God say: "Remember not the former things, nor consider the things of old. Behold, I am doing a new thing; now it springs forth, do you not perceive it?" (Isa. 43:18–19). And yet, because this "new thing"—as also the "new thing" of Christ's resurrection—is seen as the completion and fulfillment of God's past revelation and redemptive activity, it uses the language of sacred memory. Thus, when the early church sought to understand and to communicate its faith that Jesus of Nazareth is the Lord of life, it turned to the Scriptures and found that "all the promises of God find their Yes in him" (2 Cor. 1:20).

HISTORY AS HIS STORY

The New Testament sees God's story with his people and with his world focused and fulfilled in the resurrection of Jesus. To speak of God's "story"[21] is to stress the narrative character of biblical confession, whether in such Old Testament confessions of faith as Deut. 26:5ff. or in the early Christian creeds as 1 Corinthians 15. The "story" is anchored in a "history" or "salvation history," but its narration includes a transcendent quality that defies historical demonstration or proof. "Story" includes an imagery of "what no eye has seen, nor ear heard, nor the heart of man conceived" (1 Cor. 2:9). This should not surprise us. The Gospel accounts of Jesus' life and ministry cannot be reduced to demonstrable biography (e.g., the opening skies at his baptism, the Voice from heaven, the struggle with Satan, etc.). The same holds true for the resurrection of Jesus.

Anyone who has recited the Apostles' Creed knows this. To say that Jesus "suffered under Pontius Pilate, was crucified, dead, and buried" is to affirm a given history that can be demonstrated as history. But to confess that this Jesus is "Jesus Christ his only Son our Lord" who has a transcendent *before* ("conceived by the Holy Ghost, born of the Virgin Mary") and a transcendent *after* ("the third day he rose again from the dead; he ascended into heaven, and sitteth on the right hand of God the Father Almighty; from thence he shall come to judge the quick and the dead") goes far beyond historical statement.

This reminder has bearing on our reading of the New Testament. Gerald O'Collins cautions against what he calls "underbelief" and "overbelief." The former reduces the Easter message to a pictorial portrayal of what happened to disciples and not to what happened to Jesus himself. The latter interprets the New Testament texts as though the language of faith is simply prosaic and literal fact (e.g., the risen Christ eats broiled fish and thus the glorified body must have a digestive system!).[22] Xavier Léon-Dufour gives another example of "overbelief." When the Fourth Gospel portrays disciples locked in an upper room where the risen Christ comes and appears in their midst, that account says nothing about how the appearance took place. But "the modern reader hastens to supply imaginary details and builds up a whole scene: the doors are closed, *therefore* Christ passed through the closed doors. . . . To do this is to make the risen Christ a kind of Houdini."[23] Neither extreme of "underbelief" or "overbelief" does justice to the New Testament texts or to the Easter faith of the church.

Withal, the "story" of Easter, with all its transcendent language of faith, is the story of Jesus of Nazareth, whom God raised from the dead. How shall we do justice to the meaning of this "many-splendoured" center of New Testament faith in a manner permitted by the New Testament texts?

OUR APPROACH

Because Easter faith is a story of salvation we shall arrange the biblical texts in such fashion as to move from the significance of the resurrection as past event to its significance as disclosure of the future, and so to its significance for the present.

Why this order? Not a few argue that we should begin with present experience of Easter as the primary focus.[24] After all, Easter faith began as a present experience of the living Lord, from which inferences were drawn about the past and the future. Undoubtedly, such an approach does justice to the manner in which the first believers apprehended Easter. No one saw Jesus raised from the dead. That particular past was hidden from them as it is hidden from us. Men and women were encountered by the Lord, who had risen and who became present to them.

Nonetheless, the New Testament message is not content to base its Easter faith on present experience as such. Those early witnesses did not identify the Easter reality with their own coming to faith. Instead, the early Easter creed declares:

> That Christ died for our sins in accordance with the
>   scriptures,
> that he was buried,
> that he was raised on the third day in accordance with the
>   scriptures,
> and that he appeared to Cephas, then to the twelve.[25]

That is to say, the Easter message of the New Testament begins with a particular past, the crucifixion and resurrection of Jesus, which is prior to the coming to faith of his followers. This is as true of the Easter narratives and of the Easter preaching as it is true of the creedal formula. The New Testament message declares that God said Yes to Jesus by raising him from the dead, and that his Yes to Jesus is the basis of his Yes to us.

If it is necessary to begin with Easter's significance as a particular and decisive past event, why not move from the past to the present and so to its significance for the future? Would such an arrangement not be appropriate to the schema of a salvation history that affirms "Jesus Christ is the same yesterday and today and for ever" (Heb. 13:8)?

However, further reflection makes one aware that memory and hope shape the biblical interpretation of the present. For example, Rom. 1:3–4 is generally recognized to be, in whole or in part, an early formula appropriated by Paul.[26] The RSV reads: "The gospel concerning his Son, who was descended from David according to the flesh and designated Son of God in power according to the Spirit of holiness by his resurrection from the dead, Jesus Christ our Lord." The Greek text does not say "by *his* resurrection *from* the dead" but simply "by the resurrection *of* the dead." Doubtless Paul and his predecessors took this phrase about the general resurrection of the dead in the future as an abbreviation for "his" resurrection, but that illustrates how New Testament faith saw in the resurrection of Jesus the disclosure and anticipation of a future in which Jesus is "the first fruits of those who have fallen asleep" (1 Cor. 15:20).

Again, there is that puzzling apocalyptic passage in Matthew's story of the passion (Mt. 27:51–54) which speaks of earthquake, rocks rent, graves opened, and bodies of saints raised—all at the very moment of Jesus' death. That passage has a curious ambiguity, for the Evangelist adds that only "after his resurrection" did the raised saints go into the holy city. Whatever we do with this puzzling passage, we cannot avoid the conclusion that the Evangelist is portraying the death and resurrection of Jesus as the beginning of the end time (for Matthew has another earthquake at Easter).

Even in the Lukan writings, which do not portray this future as so imminently near, the disciples ask the risen Christ, "Lord, will you at this time restore the kingdom to Israel?" (Acts 1:6). At Pentecost, Peter interprets the advent of the Spirit through Joel's language of "the last days" (Acts 2:17). We have already noted Acts 4:2, where Sadducees are annoyed that the apostles were "proclaiming the resurrection from the dead—the resurrection of Jesus" (NEB). We see the same in Paul's resurrection chapter, in which he seems to ground the resurrection of Jesus on the future resurrection while at the same time basing the future resurrection on the already happened resurrection of Jesus (1 Cor. 15:12–19). That is to say, the future is seen as already penetrating the present time. Eschatology is not simply a "last chapter" of Christian belief.

Of course, eschatological enthusiasm entailed risks—whether flight from the present or illusions of premature arrival—but these risks were recognized and countered by the New Testament writers (e.g., 2 Thess. 2:2; 1 Cor. 4:8; 15:12; 2 Tim. 2:18). That such correctives were needed only underscores the extent to which memory and hope shaped the early message.[27]

For us also, memory and hope meet in the present. That is why we shall move from Easter's past and future significance to that of its significance for our present. Christians are those who "have been born anew to a living hope through the resurrection of Jesus Christ from the dead" (1 Pet. 1:3). Parenthetically, it is interesting to observe that this is also the order of Calvin's 1545 catechism.[28]

These three dimensions of the resurrection's meaning are so interrelated that it is not possible to isolate one from the other. But in the pages that follow we shall examine the extent to which this threefold pattern of significance finds expression in the New Testament traditions.

II

The Resurrection
as
Past Event

We are describing the order of the New Testament's Easter message, not the sequence of events in which it was perceived. The latter begins when disciples are encountered by the risen Lord. As John Knox put it: "The situation in the early church was not that Jesus was believed to be living because he was believed to have risen; it was rather that he was known to have risen because he was known as living."[1]

Indeed. As a past event the resurrection itself was hidden from them as it is hidden from us. No one saw Jesus raised from the dead. Even in Matthew, for all its apocalyptic description of an earthquake, of an angel of the Lord who descended to roll the stone away, and of guards who became as dead men (Mt. 28:2–4), there is no description of the resurrection itself. Such an attempt is not found until we come to the postcanonical Gospel of Peter.[2] When the Easter narratives of our Gospels proclaim the event of the resurrection, they bear witness to it as an event that has already happened and that no eye has seen. The appearances of the Lord follow the unseen event that preceded them: "The Lord has risen indeed, and has appeared to Simon" (Lk. 24:34). First the unseen event—then its attestation to Jesus' followers. This is the order of the Easter testimony, both in the creedal summaries and in the Gospel narratives.

This has important implications. To begin with disciple encounters with the risen Lord may tempt us to equate the resurrection reality with their coming to faith. Some have said that the resurrection reality is essentially a "conviction" rather than an "event."[3] Others question this distinction because a conviction is itself an event—albeit an inward event. An interpretation such as Bultmann's does not deny that Easter is an act of God, a revelation, but it is one that has its time and space only in what happened to disciples who are now enabled to understand the meaning of the cross through the eyes of faith. For Bultmann, Christ rose in the *kerygma,* in the proclaimed and received faith of his followers. Bultmann wrote:

> It is often said, most of the time in criticism, that according to my interpretation of the kerygma Jesus has risen in the kerygma. I accept this proposition. It is entirely correct, assuming that it is properly understood. It presupposes that the kerygma itself is an eschatological event, and it expresses the fact that Jesus is really present in the kerygma, that it is *his* word which involves the hearer in the kerygma. If that is the case, then all speculation concerning the modes of being of the risen Jesus, all the narratives of the empty tomb and all the Easter legends, whatever elements of historical fact they may contain, and as true as they may be in their symbolic form, are of no consequence. To believe in the Christ present in the kerygma is the meaning of the Easter faith.[4]

But this is not the whole meaning of the Easter faith. The New Testament message not only affirms that something happened and happens to Jesus' followers, it affirms that something happened to Jesus—and that what happened to him makes possible what happens to them. To say that the resurrection happened once-for-all may not forget that it happened once.

THE MESSAGE BEGINS
WITH A PARTICULAR PAST

EASTER AS HISTORY

It happened once—"once upon a time." Before we come to the New Testament data, it is useful to compare Karl Barth's approach to Easter history with that of Rudolf Bultmann's. In his early writing Barth seems to resemble what we have heard Bultmann say in the preceding pages. In 1920 he could say: "The resurrection of Christ, or his second coming, which is the same thing, is not a historical event. . . . Our concern *here* is with an event which, though it is the only real happening *in,* is not a real happening *of* history."[5] In 1921, commenting on the formula of Rom. 1:3, he wrote:

> The Resurrection is the revelation: the disclosing of Jesus as the Christ, the appearing of God, and the apprehending of God in Jesus. . . . In the Resurrection the new world of the Holy Spirit touches the old world of the flesh, but touches it as a tangent touches a circle, that is, without touching it. And, precisely because it does not touch it, it touches it as its frontier—as the new world. The Resurrection is therefore an occurrence in history, which took place outside the gates of Jerusalem in the year A.D. 30, inasmuch as it there "came to pass," was discovered and recognized. But inasmuch as the occurrence was conditioned by the Resurrection, in so far, that is, as it was not the "coming to pass," or the discovery, or the recognition, which conditioned its necessity and appearance and revelation, the Resurrection is not an event in history at all.[6]

However, in his later *Church Dogmatics* we read:

> It is essential to grasp that when the New Testament speaks of the event of Easter it really means the Easter history and Easter time. We are here in the sphere of history and time no less than in the case of the words and acts and even the death of Jesus. The event of Easter is as it were their prism through which the apostles and their communities saw the man Jesus in every as-

pect of His relation to them. . . . But this prism itself is not just a timeless idea, a kind of *a priori,* hovering as it were above the relations between Jesus and His followers. . . . No, it happened "once upon a time" that He was among them as the Resurrected. . . . Faith in the risen Lord springs from His historical manifestation, and from this as such, not from the rise of faith in Him.[7]

Barth could now speak of "a second history—or rather, the fragments of a second history—of Jesus." What once he had been content to describe as a "tangent" that touches but does not touch history has now become a "prism" created by a unique series of events.[8] Easter faith is not only a continuing reality but a unique and unrepeatable deed of God in history.

Neither the "first" nor the "second" history of Jesus allows us to write a biography. But neither do they allow us to divorce Jesus himself from a particular past of time and space.[9]

SYNTAX AND VOCABULARY

The Greek New Testament uses two verb tenses to affirm that Christ "was raised." A concordance shows that the characteristic tense is the aorist past tense, which, like the English past simple tense, indicates completed action. Sometimes the New Testament uses the Greek perfect tense, denoting an action perfected or completed in the past but whose effects are regarded as continuing into the present.

As we have said, the usual verb tense for the Easter confession is the aorist past tense: *ēgerthē* ("he has been raised"). However, in the Easter creed of 1 Corinthians 15, "that he was raised" is rendered for the perfect tense *egēgertai.* Some have argued that this is more appropriate and helpful to our interpretation of the Easter message—"that the argument moves from the present through the past to the future."[10] Yet the only times when this verb form appears with reference to the resurrection are in the creedal formulas of 1 Cor. 15:4 and 2 Tim. 2:8 (and in those subsequent verses 12–17,20, of 1 Corinthians 15 which are clearly under the influence of the creed). Nor is it all certain that the early creed intends any distinction between the perfect tense ("that he was raised") and the aorist past tense ("that Christ died for our sins"). Both clauses stress the continuing significance of what happened once as once-for-all. If the perfect tense in the creed has any theological significance, it is not to divorce the resurrection from a temporal schema but to affirm that the Christ who was raised is so forever—that death no longer can have dominion over him.

From syntax we move to vocabulary. When speaking of the resurrection of Jesus the New Testament uses two verbs synonymously: *egeirein* ("to raise") and *anistanai* ("to rise")[11]. It may or may not be that New Testament tradition progressively attributes to Christ what first was attributed to God—from "God raised him" to Christ as the one who "rose."[12] But decisive proof is lacking. As we would expect, when the verb *egeirein* is used in the active voice, God is the subject ("God raised him"). When this verb is used in the passive voice, Christ is the subject ("he was raised"). The other verb, *anistanai,* is used both transitively and intransitively. When used transitively, it is like *egeirein,* as in Acts 2:32, "This Jesus God raised up *(anestēsen)."* When used intransitively, Christ is the subject, as in Acts 17:3, "that it was necessary for the Christ to suffer and to rise *(anastēnai)* from the dead." In any case, what Christ does is inseparable from God's action in him. This is brought home in the Johannine Gospel: "For this reason the Father loves me, because I lay down my life, that I may take it again. . . . This charge I have received from my Father" (Jn. 10:17–18). Little wonder that the Easter message, "He is risen," is rendered for *ēgerthē,* which literally says, "He has been raised."

It is interesting to notice that both verbs, *egeirein* and *anistanai,* are used in the Gospel narratives of Jesus' healing ministry, both of his raising persons from death and his raising the sick.[13] For example, in the healing of the paralytic, Jesus says in each Synoptic account, "Rise" *(egeire),* but when we read that the paralytic arose, Mk. 2:12 and Mt. 9:7

use the forms *ēgerthē* and *egertheis,* while Lk. 5:25 uses *anastas.* In the story of Jairus' daughter, Jesus says, "Arise" (Mk. 5:41 and Lk. 8:54 use *egeire;* Matthew does not have the word of command, but when we read that the girl arose, Mt. 9:25 has *ēgerthē,* while Mk. 5:42 and Lk. 8:55 have *anestē).* All of this illustrates the New Testament conviction that the resurrection of Jesus completes and reveals God's whole deed in Jesus. Scott Holland put this in memorable words: "In the Resurrection it was not only the Lord who was raised from the dead. His life on earth rose with him; it was lifted up into its real light."[14] This reminds us of what Barth said in the quotation already cited: "The event of Easter is as it were their prism through which the apostles and their communities saw the man Jesus in every aspect of His relation to them."

Of particular interest is the verb "he appeared" *(ōphthē)* in the aorist past tense, a verb that occurs in many Easter confessions and narratives. Although grammatically it can be read as an aorist passive ("he was seen"), without question it should be read intransitively in the Easter references ("he appeared"). Whether or not the word has become a technical expression for the resurrection appearances,[15] it is certainly a term for revelatory disclosure. In the New Testament the word almost invariably has this sense (e.g., of angelic appearances in Lk. 1:11; 22:43; Acts 7:30; of Moses and Elijah on the Mount of Transfiguration in Mt. 17:3 and Mk. 9:4; of the risen Christ's appearances in Lk. 24:34; Acts 13:31; four times in 1 Cor. 15:5–8; and in the more cosmic disclosure portrayed in 1 Tim. 3:16). When Stephen says in Acts 7:2 that "the God of glory appeared *(ōphthē)* to our father Abraham," we are pointed to the large place that the word *ōphthē* has in the Greek Old Testament, predominantly as revelation (whether of God himself, of the angel of the Lord, or of the glory of the Lord: Gen. 12:7; 17:1; 26:2, 24; 35:9; 48:3; Ex. 3:2; 6:3; 16:10; Num. 14:10; 16:19, 42; 20:6; Judg. 6:12; 13:3; 2 Kgds. (2 Sam.) 22:11; 3 Kgds. (1 Kings) 9:2; 2 Chron. 1:7; 3:1; 7:12; cf. also Tob. 12:22). This supports the earlier contention that the closest analogy to the literary form of the resurrection appearance narratives is to be found in the theophanies of the Old Testament.

Withal, syntax and vocabulary make plain that the New Testament message of the resurrection does not divorce the event itself (and the appearances that follow) from a particular past of time and space.

THE THIRD DAY

Let us begin with time. Granting that Luke's "forty days" represents only one strain of New Testament witness, we may take this as a symbolic pointer to the unique and unrepeatable character of the whole Easter time. But what of "the third day"?

"The third day" is prominent in the New Testament message. It occurs explicitly in the Easter testimony itself. The creed in 1 Corinthians 15 affirms "that he was raised on the third day in accordance with the scriptures." In Luke's resurrection chapter the risen Lord says to his disciples, "Thus it is written, that the Christ should suffer and on the third day rise from the dead" (Lk. 24:46). The phrase occurs in Peter's Easter preaching to Cornelius: "God raised him on the third day and made him manifest" (Acts 10:40).

The phrase occurs also in passages that clearly reflect the Easter faith. When the Emmaus travelers speak of the crucifixion to the yet unrecognized Christ they say, "Yes, and besides all this, it is now the third day since this happened" (Lk. 24:21). In the Johannine account of the cleansing of the Temple, Jesus says: " 'Destroy this temple, and in three days I will raise it up.' ... When therefore he was raised from the dead, his disciples remembered that he had said this; and they believed the scripture and the word which Jesus had spoken" (Jn. 2:20, 22).

To this data we must add the three passion sayings of the Synoptic Gospels in which Jesus speaks of the approaching death of the Son of Man and of his rising again "after three days" (Mk. 8:31; 9:31; 10:34; the parallels are in Mt. 16:21; 17:23; 20:19 and in Lk. 9:22 and 18:33 as "on the third day"). Since Jewish usage reckons a part of a day as a whole day, there is no essential difference between "after three days" and "on the third day."[16] This is evident in the words of the Jewish authorities to Pilate: "Sir, we remember how that imposter said, while he was still alive, 'After three days I will rise again.' Therefore order the sepulchre to be made secure until the third day" (Mt. 27:63–64). This equivalence between the two phrases also enables us to understand how Mt. 12:40 can utilize the sign of Jonah (Jon. 1:17 as Christological testimony: "For as Jonah was three days and three nights in the belly of the whale [sea monster], so will the Son of man be three days and three nights in the heart of the earth").

How shall we understand "the third day"? Since several of the passages cited link "the third day" with Scripture, many scholars have sought its origin in the early church's interpretation of the Old Testament. As we have seen in the preceding chapter, the prevailing disposition has been to turn to Hos. 6:2, Christologically interpreted ("After two days he will revive us; on the third day he will raise us up, that we may live before him"). We know that the later rabbinic interpretation linked this text with the end of the age—and early Christianity saw in the resurrection of Jesus the dawning of the end time. Yet, as we have also noted, this text is never cited in the New Testament. Moreover, the early creed says "in accordance with the scriptures" (plural). Thus, other scholars have noted how often the Old Testament associates "the third day" with Israel's salvation history. For example, "On the third day Abraham lifted up his eyes and saw the place" (Gen. 22:4) where he was to sacrifice Isaac—and this day brought the preservation of the promised son and a blessing for Abraham. The later Jewish midrash (commentaries seeking a deeper meaning of the text) cite seven texts to show that God never leaves the righteous in distress for more than three days.[17] Since Genesis 22 is used in a resurrection context in the New Testament (Acts 3:25f.; Heb.

11:17ff.), it is certainly as possible that this reference to "the third day" was noticed in the formation of New Testament tradition, as the Hosea text might have been. If God did not leave righteous Abraham in distress for more than three days, how much less would he have left "the Holy and Righteous One" (Acts 3:14) in distress for more than three days.

Nor is this all. "Three days" or "the third day" occurs frequently in the salvation history of Israel: in the story of the exodus (Ex. 15:22), in the revelation at Sinai (Ex. 19:10f.), in the story of the conquest (Josh. 20:30), in the anointing of Israel's first king (1 Sam. 9:19f.), in the return from exile (Ezra 8:15, 32). On this basis, E. L. Bode concludes that, instead of seeking to explain "in accordance with the scriptures" through a single verse, we should account for it through a general Old Testament motif, reinforced by the later midrash and targum of Jewish interpretation, "that the third day is the day of divine salvation, deliverance, and manifestation."[18]

All this may be true. Yet one wonders whether the origin of "the third day" for Jesus' resurrection is sufficiently accounted for on this basis. Since not one of these texts is specifically a resurrection text, it is more likely that historical tradition of Easter sent the early church to its Scriptures in order to see that this "third day" was indeed "in accordance with the scriptures." Hans von Campenhausen's words are worth considering:

> It must, then, be assumed that "the third day" was probably somehow already given before it could be discovered in the Old Testament and taken over into the confession. . . . Thus, at the very least, we must allow the possibility that the statement about the "third" day was meant to be historical.[19]

Evidently Paul understood the resurrection appearances as historically sequential in 1 Cor. 15:3–8 ("then . . . then . . . then . . . last of all"). In all likelihood he, as the formula before him, understood "died . . . was buried . . . was raised on the third day" as equally sequential historically. Certainly, of itself, "the third day" did not elicit Easter faith, for in Luke's Emmaus story disheartened followers say of the crucifixion, "Yes, and besides all this, it is now the third day since this happened" (Lk. 24:21).

Others have looked for the origin of "the third day" in the passion predictions of Jesus as we have these in the Gospels. Although the present shape of these passion sayings (Mk. 8:31; 9:31; 10:33–34, and parallels) is undoubtedly colored by the Easter faith that pervades the gospel tradition, this does not mean that the nucleus of these sayings cannot go back to Jesus himself. Without doubt, he who set his face to go to Jerusalem did so in full awareness of the danger that awaited him there—but also in the confidence that God was with him and would be with him to vindicate his mission. In all likelihood, the original meaning of his words "after three days" or "on the third day" was a figurative way of saying "speedily, in a little while," rather than an exact prediction. We think of his analogous reply to those who warn him about Herod. "Go and tell that fox, 'Behold, I cast out demons and perform cures today and tomorrow, and the third day I finish my course. Nevertheless I must go on my way today and tomorrow and the day following; for it cannot be that a prophet should perish away from Jerusalem" (Lk. 13:32–33).

We do violence to the full humanity of Jesus if we suppose that he knew in advance exactly how and when God would vindicate his life of utter obedience. The Easter affirmations of "the third day" are certainly congruous with the life and word of Jesus. Yet the gospel data do not lead us to conclude that the Easter affirmation of "the third day" could have attained its central place in the tradition simply on the basis of Jesus' prior words—any more than they could have done so on the basis of Old Testament interpretation.

Still others have sought the origin of Easter's "third day" in the early church's liturgical celebration. This is not persuasive, for the early church did not begin with a new calendar of worship. Indeed, if the Easter time references have any liturgical overtones, these are to be found in "the first day of the week" with which all four Gospels begin their Easter chapters. By the time our Gospels were written, the first day of the week had become the day of Christian assembly (cf. 1 Cor. 16:2; Acts 20:7; Rev. 1:10). We cannot here trace the origin of the Christian Sunday, as Willy Rordorf has sought to do in his volume *Sunday.* He is surely right in asserting: "The selection of Sunday as the day for worship must in some way be connected with the resurrection of Jesus."[20]

But how are we to understand the causal relationship between the Easter tradition and the day of Christian worship? Do the Gospels place their accounts of Easter morning on the first day of the week because their accounts reflect early worship? Or was it the Easter events that determined the subsequent time of early worship? If there is liturgical symbolism in the Gospel tradition of the burial and resurrection of Jesus, we should look for it in the way in which the Sabbath was transcended. In the Old Testament cultus, the Sabbath "rest" celebrated the completion of God's creation. Easter celebrates God's new creation on the first day of the week.

Pointing to structural and thematic correlations in Mt. 27:57 to 28:20, C. H. Giblin[21] has suggested that the narrative contains the ultimate irony—that Jesus is indeed "lord of the sabbath" (cf. Mt. 12:8). In Matthew, both opponents (27:63f.) and followers (16:21; 17:22f.; 20:18f.) have heard the passion predictions with their promise of a third day, but only disciples who have encountered the living Lord are able to grasp the truth that "something greater than the temple is here" and that "the Son of man is lord of the sabbath." In any case, if "the third day" had its origin in liturgy, we would expect that the Easter chapters would have begun with such expressions as "very early on the third day."[22]

These considerations lead us to conclude that "the third day" has its Easter origin in historical memory, whether from the discovery of the empty tomb or from the first appearances. That this "third day" found its confirmation and interpretation in Scriptural-theological reflection we do not doubt. But the phrase bears its own witness that Easter has its own correlate of time.

THE EMPTY TOMB

Space as well as time is a correlate of Easter as past event. Despite redactional differences in the testimony of the four Gospels, the empty grave is the common feature in all four.

Because scholarship has often tended to make the early creed of 1 Corinthians 15 the norm for interpreting the earliest Easter faith (and because that creed does not mention the empty grave), it is often assumed that the grave narrative represents a later legendary accretion to support and to strengthen Easter faith. In other words, the grave narrative functions as a later apologetic for Easter faith. This view assumes that the earliest faith was marked by "heavenly radiance" visions of the risen Lord rather than by appearances that could be termed "bodily."

Such an interpretation points out that Paul, who says nothing of an empty grave and who links his own resurrection encounter with those of the earliest witnesses, says that "flesh and blood cannot inherit the kingdom of God, nor does the perishable inherit the imperishable" (1 Cor. 15:50). If this is said about our own future resurrection, would it not be said of Christ himself? Even if Paul's Pharisaic background included belief in a bodily resurrection, this would be "a spiritual body" and not like the Lukan portrayal of a risen Jesus who says: "Handle me, and see; for a spirit has not flesh and bones as you see that I have" (Lk. 24:39).

Accordingly, in various ways it has been suggested that the story of the empty grave is a later paradigm to support and to strengthen Easter faith.[23] Long ago, Maurice Goguel suggested that the story began from the deduction that "the grave is empty because the Lord is risen" and grew in importance until it was turned around to say that "the Lord is risen because the grave is empty."[24] Others suggest that the stress on "bodily" resurrection was greatly stimulated by early

Christian reflection on Ps. 16:10, a text cited twice by Luke (Acts 2:27; 13:35).[25] Such Scriptural apologetic would become more prominent when joined with the need to meet the charge of opponents that disciples had stolen the body of Jesus, a concern evidenced in the grave narratives (Mt. 27: 62–66; 28:11–15; cf. Jn. 20:2, 13, 15). If all this is so, then the resurrection itself cannot and need not be located in a given past which has its own correlates of space and time.[26]

To be sure, the formula in 1 Corinthians 15 does not include any reference to the empty grave. The phrase "that he was buried" may imply that he was raised from the grave, but its force in the formula is simply to underscore "that Christ died [really died] for our sins." As for the Pauline statement that "flesh and blood cannot inherit the kingdom of God," this must not be taken as suggesting immortality rather than resurrection, for Paul stresses the reality of a "spiritual body." Indeed, the whole discussion of 1 Cor. 15:35ff. about a "spiritual body" is perfectly compatible with his statement in Phil. 3:21 that the Lord "will change [transform] our lowly body to be like his glorious body." For that matter, the Lukan and Johannine portrayals of the "bodily" resurrection of a Lord who shows disciples the marks of the cross do not suggest resuscitation of the old body. The suddenness and mystery of his appearings and departures indicate that these Evangelists bear their own witness to the Lord's "glorious body."

Nor is it likely that the story of the grave has its origin in the early church's reflection on Ps. 16:10 ("For thou dost not give me up to Sheol, or let thy godly one see the Pit"). It is Luke only who cites this verse (Acts 2:27ff.; 13:35)—not to argue for an empty grave but to show that the messianic promise is fulfilled in the risen Jesus and not in David, whose "tomb is with us to this day" (Acts 2:29). Of course Luke himself attests the empty grave (Luke 24), but the speeches of Acts do not use the psalm to refer to the narrative of the grave.[27]

Today there is a growing consensus in New Testament

scholarship that the tradition of the empty grave is early tradition, not a late addition. How shall we account for the narrative's origin?

Some scholars suggest that the grave story combines historical memory with an early cultic celebration of Easter through an annual pilgrimage to the tomb of Jesus.[28] However, we have no data for an early cultic interest in the grave. Such interest finds later expression in the days of Constantine with the erection of a Church of the Holy Sepulchre. Moreover, if Mark was written shortly before the destruction of Jerusalem, and if the other Gospels were written after that destruction,[29] one may ask whether cultic interest in holy places provided a likely setting for the narrative. If some scholars suggest that cultic interest is reflected in the angelic proclamation, "See the place where they laid him" (Mk. 16:6), others can point to an apparent disavowal of such interest in the words, "Why do you seek the living among the dead?" (Lk. 24:5).

Form critics agree that while much of the gospel tradition first circulated as separate and self-contained units, the earliest continuous "whole" piece is the passion narrative. Ulrich Wilckens[30] argues that already at a very early time the story of the empty grave was an integral part of the passion narrative. Despite criticism of his view,[31] it merits serious consideration. After all, it is hardly possible that the passion narrative, so central in early preaching and worship, could have concluded with the burial without bearing its own witness that the cross was not a defeat.

The structure of the passion narrative lends support to this claim. That narrative (doubtless finding its earliest written form in Mark) has been shaped by the Old Testament psalms of the righteous sufferer. The cry, "My God, my God, why hast thou forsaken me?" (Ps. 22:1; Mk. 15:34; Mt. 27:46), only epitomizes the influence of these psalms on the narrative. It is hardly likely that the passion narrative itself would say less than the psalms that shape it. The appendix to this chapter will illustrate how all the psalms reflected in the passion narrative portray the sufferer's cry to God—and the question of these psalms is precisely the question posed by the death of Jesus. Will God forsake his righteous one? Think of it! God's righteous one delivered into the hands of his enemies (Mk. 14:41). But these same psalms are more than cries for God's vindication. Every one of them is an affirmation and assurance that the righteous God vindicates righteousness. It is inconceivable that the passion narrative would do less than the Scriptures that shape it. That narrative not only includes a centurion's confession that Jesus is the Son of God. It includes a burial that leads us quickly to something more than an empty grave—it leads us to the angelic proclamation: "Do not be amazed; you seek Jesus of Nazareth, who was crucified. He has risen, he is not here; see the place where they laid him" (Mk. 16:6). That is to say, the passion narrative closes not with a question but with a divine answer.

Other considerations support the contention that the grave story is not an apologetic addition but an integral part of the earliest witness. It is hardly plausible that a later apologetic would have chosen women rather than apostles as the first witnesses to an empty tomb. While two Gospels bring apostles also to the tomb (Lk. 24:12; Jn. 20:2ff.), these do so only after the women have told their story.

Critical study has shown that originally the grave story and the appearance stories circulated independently of each other. Both in Matthew and in John, where the appearance tradition is woven into the narrative of the tomb, the literary "seams" are evident.[32]

Over against the hypothesis that the story of the grave is a later effort to demonstrate and "prove" the resurrection, the Gospel accounts do not make it so. Of itself the empty grave does not elicit faith. The reality of the resurrection is not open to human discovery but is only revealed when the risen Lord makes himself known to his followers. The grave is a pointer rather than a proof. Indeed, it is not really correct to speak of the "discovery" of the empty grave. In the narratives, and especially in Mark, the women are confronted with the wonder of a stone rolled away and with the Easter message of the angel interpreter before they see that the body of Jesus is not in the tomb.

Accordingly, the only satisfying conclusion is that the empty grave is itself part and parcel of the early Easter history. Whatever the final verdict will be about the Turin Shroud, it has renewed historical attention to the Gospel narratives of the burial and the empty grave.[33] Withal, by itself the empty grave will never demonstrate the reality of the resurrection. After all, even Mary Magdalene could suppose that someone had taken the body away (Jn. 20:2, 13). When linked with the angelic message, the empty grave becomes a pointer to the greater reality which is revealed in the Lord's appearing.

"See the place where they laid him." Place as well as time is a correlate of the Easter message.

We have not tried to undertake here a detailed history-of-tradition analysis of the Gospels in order to probe behind the interpretations of the individual Evangelists. Nor have we tried to reconstruct the sequence of Easter events with their varied settings in Jerusalem and Galilee.[34] We are concerned with the Easter message. That message insists that the resurrection of Jesus occurred in a particular past and that this past event is absolutely decisive for faith.

Accordingly, from the affirmation of this particular past we turn to its meaning for faith.

THE FIRST EASTER
AS REVELATION

A psalm often cited in the New Testament in various contexts, including a reference to the resurrection, exemplifies the Easter message. "The stone which the builders rejected has become the head of the corner. This is the Lord's doing; it is marvelous in our eyes." (Ps. 118:22–23; Mt. 21:42; Mk. 12:10; Lk. 20:17; Acts 4:11; 1 Pet. 2:7).

Indeed, that is why the resurrection itself cannot be described; it can only be confessed. What eye has not seen, God has revealed. Easter is the revelation of God. Little wonder that in many Easter confessions God himself is the subject. For example:

> It will be reckoned to us who believe in him that raised from the dead Jesus our Lord. (Rom. 4:24)

> And believe in your heart that God raised him from the dead. (Rom. 10:9)

> To serve a living and true God, and to wait for his Son from heaven, whom he raised from the dead, Jesus. (1 Thess. 1:9–10)

> Through him [Jesus] you have confidence in God, who raised him from the dead and gave him glory, so that your faith and hope are in God. (1 Pet. 1:21)

No eye has seen the resurrection, but men and women saw the resurrected one. Jesus is the revealer as well as the revelation. "Jesus revealed himself *(ephanerōsen)* again to the disciples" (Jn. 21:1); "he presented himself *(parestēsen)* alive after his passion" (Acts 1:3). "He appeared" *(ōphthē)*. We have noted already that this last verb is *par excellence* the verb of revelatory disclosure. The risen Lord was not discovered. He revealed himself. Luke's Emmaus story makes this plain: "Their eyes were kept from recognizing him . . . and [then] their eyes were opened and they recognized him" (Lk. 24: 16,31).

Luke puts in narrative form what is common to the united witness of the New Testament. The epistle to the Ephesians begins with a prayer "that the God of our Lord Jesus Christ, the Father of glory, may give you a spirit of wisdom and of revelation in the knowledge of him, having the eyes of your hearts enlightened, that you may know what is the hope to which he has called you . . . and what is the immeasurable greatness of his power in us who believe, according to the working of his great might which he accomplished in Christ when he raised him from the dead" (Eph. 1:17–20).

What does the first Easter reveal? What did God do when he raised Jesus from the dead?

GOD VINDICATED JESUS

Easter was God's Yes to the ministry of Jesus. As the appendix to this chapter will show, the vindication theme links the narrative of the empty grave with the passion narrative. The theme of vindication is anticipated in the Gospel narratives of Jesus' ministry. His miracles gave the lie to those who said that he cast out demons by Beelzebul (Mk. 3:22ff.). As we have seen, the passion sayings express Jesus' own trust that God will vindicate his mission. Again, he said that "whoever is ashamed of me and of my words, . . . of him will the Son of man also be ashamed, when he comes in the glory of his Father with the holy angels" (Mk. 8:38 and parallels). The imagery of the vindicated Son of Man calls to mind Daniel's vision of the Son of Man vindicated after humiliation and oppression (Dan. 7:13f.). Nowhere is the trust that the defendant will become the judge disclosed more strikingly than in the scene before Caiaphas when Jesus says, "You will see the Son of man seated at the right hand of Power, and coming with the clouds of heaven" (Mk 14:62 and parallels). While this coming points to the future, it bears also on the coming at Easter, for Daniel's vision is reflected in the closing scene in Matthew where the Lord of Easter says, "All authority in heaven and on earth has been given to me" (Mt. 28:18).

In the Fourth Gospel, Jesus' whole ministry is illumined by the Easter light. "The Father judges no one, but has given all judgment to the Son. . . . For as the Father has life in himself, so he has granted the Son also to have life in himself, and has given him authority to execute judgment, because he is the Son of man" (Jn. 5:22, 26–27). When Jesus is arrested, the defendant is already the judge, for those who come to arrest him "drew back and fell to the ground" before his majestic "I am" (*egō eimi,* Jn. 18:6). In John's portrayal Pilate seems more the defendant than Jesus.

The note of vindication is prominent in the Lukan writings. Luke says that when the centurion saw what had taken place at the cross, "he praised God, and said, 'Certainly this man was innocent!' " (Lk. 23:47), and Luke's Easter chapter reveals how God reversed the injustice inflicted on Jesus. The vindication theme is prominent in Luke's second volume, especially in the recurrent antithesis of the early preaching: "You killed him . . . but God raised him" (Acts 2:23; 3:15; 4:10; 5:30). This theme continues when the Gospel moves beyond Jerusalem: "They killed him . . . but God raised him" (Acts 10:39ff.; 13:29ff.). Nor is this limited to the antithetic formulas. Jesus, unjustly condemned, has been vindicated. The defendant has become the judge,[35] "ordained (*hōrismenos*) by God to be judge of the living and the dead" (Acts 10:42). At Athens, Paul declares that God "has fixed a day on which he will judge the world in righteousness by a man whom he has appointed (*hōrisen*), and of this he has given assurance to all men by raising him from the dead" (Acts 17:31).

The note of vindication is apparent in the early formula of Rom. 1:3–4, for the one who was descended from David according to the flesh has been designated (*horisthentos*) Son of God in power through the resurrection. Paul himself sees the resurrection as God's vindication of Jesus and as the pledge of judgment (1 Thess. 1:10).

In the Apocalypse the theme is naturally prominent. "Fear not, I am the first and the last, and the living one; I died, and behold I am alive for evermore, and I have the keys of Death and Hades" (Rev. 1:17–18).

Common to all these examples is the theme that God has reversed the injustice inflicted on Jesus. God has pronounced his righteous judgment. Human faithlessness cannot nullify the faithfulness of God. "Let God be true though every man be false" (Rom. 3:4). God has pronounced the crucified Jesus as the righteous one.

The words "vindicate" and "vindication" do not appear in the older translations, such as the KJV, but they are appropriate renderings of several Hebrew and Greek words used when the text emphasizes the successful establishment of a person's cause as just. For example, in one of the psalms that is quoted in the New Testament and that is reflected in the passion narrative, the righteous sufferer cries: "Vindicate me, O Lord, my God, according to thy righteousness" (Ps. 35:24, rendered "Judge me" in KJV).[36] Again, Jesus concluded the parable of the unjust judge by saying: "And will not God vindicate his elect, who cry to him day and night? . . . I tell you, he will vindicate them speedily" (Lk. 18:7–8. NEB also renders "vindicate," while KJV renders "avenge"; Moffatt and Jerusalem Bible render "see justice done"). Easter ensures that Jesus' confidence in God's vindicating righteousness was not misplaced.

Before leaving the vindication theme, we may note two consequences. The first finds frequent expression. Just as in Daniel 7 the kingdom is given not only to the Son of Man but to "the saints of the Most High" who seem to be included in the Son of Man, so the New Testament links Jesus' vindication with that of his followers. One thinks of the Lukan passage in which Jesus says to the Twelve, "You are those who have continued with me in my trials; and I assign to you, as my Father assigned to me, a kingdom, that you may eat and drink at my table in my kingdom, and sit on thrones judging the twelve tribes of Israel" (Lk. 22:28–30). "Truly, I say to you, in the new world, when the Son of man shall sit on his glorious throne, you who have followed me will also sit on twelve thrones, judging the twelve tribes of Israel" (Mt. 19:28). Paul reminds his readers in Corinth that "the saints will judge the world" (1 Cor. 6:2) in order to shame them. That the saints will be vindicated with their Lord is a recurring theme in the Apocalypse (cf. Rev. 2:26; 5:10; 20:4).

That the vindicated Christ will vindicate his followers is a common theme. Only seldom, however, do we find that the vindicated Jesus will vindicate his opponents. The antithetic formulas in Acts do not express this, even though Luke does suggest it in the prayer of Jesus for his enemies (Lk. 23:34) and in the parallel prayer of Stephen (Acts 7:60). C. F. D. Moule finds that this note is clearly expressed only in Romans 5 and in 1 John 2:1, reminding us that in the Old Testament also it is seldom expressed (cf. Isaiah 53 and perhaps in Moses' readiness to be blotted out for his recalcitrant people in Ex. 32:32). As Moule suggests, this indicates the limitations of the imagery of vindication unless it is joined with the imagery of redemption. He concludes:

> It may be precisely because Jesus left behind him no explicit reinterpretation of the vindicated one in terms of the redeeming one, but relied on his own life and the power of his Risen Presence in the Holy Spirit rather than on a tradition of teaching, that the early church, with mighty exceptions like St Paul, often missed the point.[37]

Be that as it may, Easter faith declares that the God of righteousness has vindicated his righteous one. His Yes to Jesus is the basis of his Yes to us.

GOD EXALTED JESUS

The preceding discussion has indicated how closely the theme of vindication is linked with that of exaltation. In the first chapter we noted the many hymnic passages that use the language of exaltation. If Phil. 2:6–11 is a classic example of a hymnody of exaltation that does not use the vocabulary of resurrection, the doxology of Eph. 1:19–23 is a classic example of how the language of exaltation can be joined with that of resurrection:

> and what is the immeasurable greatness of his power in us who believe, according to the working of his great might which he accomplished in Christ when he raised him from the dead and made him sit at his right hand in the heavenly places, far above all rule and authority and power and dominion, and above every name that is named, not only in this age but also in that which

is to come; and he has put all things under his feet and has made him the head over all things for the church, which is his body, the fulness of him who fills all in all.

Such language not only witnesses to a defendant whose cause has been vindicated; it is the language of enthronement, drawing especially from such royal psalms as Ps. 2 and 110. Jesus Christ is the messianic king. (Eph. 1:22 links Ps. 110 with Ps. 8:6) More than that, he is Lord of all, the Son of God in power, now and forever "at the right hand of God."

Every vocabulary has its limitations (as we saw in the imagery of vindication). The language of resurrection maintains the Easter confession that the cross and the resurrection are inseparable, that the risen one is none other than Jesus of Nazareth. Yet resurrection must not be confused with resuscitation to mortal life. The Gospel stories of the raising of Jairus' daughter, or of the widow's son at Nain, or of Lazarus, are not analogies for the resurrection of Jesus. In this respect, the language of exaltation has an advantage because it indicates the transformation and glory of the risen Christ. Nonetheless, without the language of resurrection, exaltation could easily suggest a timeless and distant Lord instead of Christ crucified and risen.

In this connection the Johannine theology is fascinating. The Evangelist does not forsake the language of resurrection (e.g., Jn. 2:22; 10:18; 11:23; 21:14). His Easter narratives stress the "bodily" resurrection of Jesus as much as those of Luke. Yet Johannine theology more often uses the language of exaltation. John frequently employs the verb "to ascend" *(anabainein).* "No one has ascended into heaven but he who descended from heaven, the Son of man" (3:13). "What if you were to see the Son of man ascending where he was before?" (6:62). To Mary, Jesus says, "Do not hold me, for I have not yet ascended to the Father" (20:17). John also uses the verb "to lift up" *(hypsoun).* "And as Moses lifted up the serpent in the wilderness, so must the Son of man be lifted up" (3:14). "Now is the judgment of this world, now shall the ruler of this world be cast out; and I, when I am lifted up from the earth, will draw all men to myself" (12:31–32). This "lifting up" refers to both cross and resurrection.

John is particularly fond of the words "to glorify" *(doxazein)* and "glory" *(doxa)*. "Now is the Son of man glorified, and in him God is glorified; if God is glorified in him, God will also glorify him in himself, and glorify him at once" (13:31). "Father, the hour has come; glorify thy Son that the Son may glorify thee. . . . And now, Father, glorify thou me in thy own presence with the glory which I had with thee before the world was" (17:1,5). Yet the Johannine theology of preexistence and incarnation never loses sight of the "flesh" of Jesus or the centrality of his cross. The hour of his crucifixion is the hour of his glory. This does not mean that the resurrection itself becomes expendable. It means rather that the language of exaltation cannot be taken as a timeless glory. "Jesus came and stood among them and said to them, 'Peace be with you.' When he had said this, he showed them his hands and his side" (20:19–20).

In contrast to the Fourth Gospel and to the general pattern of the New Testament in which vindication and exaltation are brought together, Luke's forty days and his ascension story seem to distinguish resurrection as vindication from ascension as exaltation. Yet Luke is not as far removed from John as is often maintained. His Easter narratives are closer to John's than to those of Matthew and Mark. The risen Jesus meets his followers with the same suddenness and mystery. His credentials are the marks of the cross: "See my hands and my feet, that it is I myself" (Lk. 24:39; cf. Jn. 20:20). Although Luke narrates an ascension into heaven, the only place where the noun *analēmpsis* ("ascension") occurs in the New Testament is in Luke 9:51, where it is linked with the coming cross: "As the time approached when he was to be taken up to heaven, he set his face resolutely toward Jerusalem" (NEB). There are significant differences, of course. In John the hour of the passion is already the hour of glory, while in Luke the risen Lord says to his followers,

"Was the Messiah not bound to suffer thus before entering upon his glory?" (Lk. 24:26, NEB).

Still, despite the narrative of the ascension, the speeches of Acts come close to equating resurrection and exaltation: "The God of our fathers raised Jesus whom you killed. ... God exalted him at his right hand as Leader and Savior" (Acts 5:30–31). Luke does not visualize the forty days as though these represent a quasi return to former life which must give way to glory. The Lord who appears to his followers is already the one who comes and goes in all of the mystery of his new life. The ascension, then, is not a change from earthly life to heavenly glory. Rather, it is Luke's way of saying that the Easter appearances have ended—his way of saying what Paul's Easter creed says in the words "last of all."

The language of ascent suggests not only a royal enthronement but a cultic ascent to the Temple. Both images are drawn from Israel's tradition. Thus it will not surprise us that the cultic and priestly imagery of ascent should find its place in the New Testament. Here one thinks especially of the portrayal of Jesus as the great High Priest in the epistle to the Hebrews. Except for the closing ascription (Heb. 13:20), this epistle consistently uses the language of ascent rather than that of resurrection. "When he had made purification for sins, he sat down at the right hand of the Majesty on high" (Heb. 1:3). As Ps. 110 provided the royal imagery of "the right hand," it also provided the priestly imagery of this epistle: "You are a priest for ever after the order of Melchizedek" (Ps. 110: 4; Heb. 5:6,10; 6:20; 7:3,17,21). In Jesus "we have such a high priest, one who is seated at the right hand of the throne of the Majesty in heaven, a minister in the sanctuary and the true tent" (Heb. 8:1–2). As High Priest "he entered once for all into the Holy Place" (9:12). "But when Christ had offered for all time a single sacrifice for sins, he sat down at the right hand of God" (10:12).

Easter declares that God has exalted Jesus.

GOD EFFECTED OUR REDEMPTION

For a long time Western theology was so exclusively preoccupied with the atoning death of Christ that it did not sufficiently express the New Testament insistence that cross and resurrection together constitute the great redemption.[38] "Who is to condemn? Is it Christ Jesus, who died, yes, who was raised from the dead, . . . who indeed intercedes for us?" (Rom. 8:34).

When we examined the language of resurrection we noted that the same words for "raise" and "rise" used at Easter are used in the Synoptic miracle stories such as the healing of the paralytic. Significantly, the point of that healing is found in Jesus' words: " 'But that you may know that the Son of man has authority on earth to forgive sins'—he said to the paralytic—'I say to you, rise . . .' " (Mk 2:10–11 and parallels). T. F. Torrance comments that the early church "not only understood the incident as falling within the sphere of the power of the resurrection, but understood the relation of the resurrection to the forgiveness of sins after the pattern of these two words of Jesus. . . . In other words, it is in the resurrection of Jesus that all that God had to say about our forgiveness, and all that Jesus had said about forgiveness, became actualized in the same sphere of reality as that to which we belong."[39]

Easter as Restored Fellowship

In the Gospel narratives, Easter portrays restored fellowship and communion after disciple failure and flight. Although Mark has no resurrection appearance stories, he gives the promise: "But go, tell his disciples and Peter that he is going before you to Galilee; there you will see him, as he told you" (Mk. 16:7). The words "as he told you" point us back to Mark's description of the last evening: "You will all fall away; for it is written, 'I will strike the shepherd, and the sheep will be scattered.' But after I am raised up, I will go before you to Galilee" (Mk. 14:27–28). Whatever else this means, it pledges a restoration of communion with those who had abandoned Jesus in his hour of need.

But why the particular mention of Peter? Were this in Matthew, we might link it especially with the foundational place of Peter in the early church (Mt. 16:17f.). Here, however, the promise to the disciples "and Peter," who are to see Jesus "as he told you," recalls Mk. 14:27ff. Those words not only spoke of all the disciples falling away but added a prediction of Peter's denial. Thus the angelic message of Easter morning includes a promise of restored communion, a relationship that had been broken by disciple failure. If the narratives of Easter do not speak explicitly of disciple penitence and of reconciliation, the substance is surely there.[40]

Matthew's narratives include reminders that Easter made worship possible (Mt. 28:9, 17), and they close with the promise of Emmanuel with which this Gospel had begun: "And lo, I am with you always, to the close of the age" (28:20; cf. 1:23 and 18:20).

In Luke's Emmaus narrative, Cleopas and his companion "had hoped that he was the one to redeem Israel" (Lk. 24:21). The risen Lord not only opened to them the Scriptures, but at table he was known to them in the breaking of bread. The same emphasis recurs in Luke's second volume, for the first witnesses "ate and drank with him after he rose from the dead" (Acts 10:41). When the risen Lord appeared to disciples in Jerusalem it was to open their minds to understand the Scriptures so "that repentance and forgiveness of sins should be preached in his name to all nations" (Lk. 24:47). Luke may not develop a theology of atonement but he certainly emphasizes that the preaching of repentance and forgiveness of sins was part of the apostolic message of the resurrection (e.g., Acts 2:37f.; 5:31f.; 26:16f.).[41] The first healing miracle (Acts 3) parallels Jesus' healing of the paralytic and becomes an occasion for preaching the resurrection.

John's resurrection narratives include reminders that Easter has brought restored fellowship. Mary recognized her

Lord when he spoke her name (Jn. 20:16), recalling how the Good Shepherd knows his sheep by name (10:3) and lays down his life for them. The appearance of Jesus to the disciples portrays the joy of restored communion. "Then the disciples rejoiced when they saw him" (20:20; RSV renders this too weakly as "were glad," for the scene recalls the promise that sorrow will turn to joy because "I will see you again and your hearts will rejoice, . . . that your joy may be full" in 16:22, 24). In the Johannine epilogue (ch. 21) Peter is asked three times whether he loves Jesus. This is undoubtedly a restoration of fellowship for one who had denied Jesus three times.

Easter as Justification

Restored communion with Jesus is reconciliation with God in and through Jesus. Paul portrays this in terms of justification. This finds its classic expression in the words: "It will be reckoned to us who believe in him that raised from the dead Jesus our Lord, who was put to death for our trespasses and raised for our justification" (Rom. 4:24–25). Torrance in right in complaining that when "the Protestant doctrine of justification is formulated only in terms of forensic imputation of righteousness or the non-imputation of sins in such a way as to avoid saying that to justify is to make righteous, it is the resurrection that is being by-passed."[42] Justification is not an impersonal transaction. It is bound up with a conception of justification as a real union with the living Christ in whom God has acted creatively not only to vindicate Jesus' own righteousness but to create in him a new community of righteousness.

Paul saw God's justifying and atoning act in the cross *and* resurrection. As Markus Barth puts it:

It may have looked as if the Son had labored in vain for the evildoers, but his resurrection signifies that his works were justified, as he himself is justified. His death was a prayer. His resurrection is the answer: the intercession has been heard. His speaking-for-us is not in vain. God enthrones the speaker-for-us at his right hand so that Christ will always have God's ear.[43]

Easter and Christ's Intercession

The preceding words of Markus Barth remind us how closely justification is linked with intercession. Paul develops this in Romans 8. "Who shall bring any charge against God's elect? It is God who justifies; who is to condemn? Is it Christ Jesus, who died, yes, who was raised from the dead, who is at the right hand of God, who indeed intercedes for us?" (Rom. 8:33–34. While the RSV puts the last verse as a rhetorical question, it is more probably a confessional statement).

Luke portrays Christ's intercession in the passion narrative, both in the prayer, "Father, forgive them; for they know not what they do" (Lk. 23:34) and in the words to the dying thief, "Truly, I say to you, today you will be with me in Paradise" (23:43). Easter faith assures that Jesus' prayer is heard.

In the Fourth Gospel intercession finds expression most forcibly in the great prayer of ch. 17: "I am praying for them. . . . And I am coming to thee. . . . I do not pray for these only. . . . I made known to them thy name, and I will make it known" (Jn. 17:9,11,20,26). The prayer concludes the farewell discourses in which Jesus assures his disciples that he goes to the Father to prepare a place for them (14:3). When Thomas asks, "How can we know the way?" Jesus replies, "I am the way, and the truth, and the life" (14:5–6). Long ago Augustine wrote:

> Walk by him the man and thou comest to God. By him thou goest, to him thou goest. Look not for any way except himself by which to come to him. For if he had not vouchsafed to be the way we should all have gone astray. Therefore he became the way by which thou shouldst come. I do not say to thee, seek the way. The way itself has come to thee: arise and walk.[44]

Intercession means that "the man for others" will always be such. In the Johannine epistle intercession is expressed in terms of advocacy: "If any one does sin, we have an advocate *(paraklētos)* with the Father, Jesus Christ the righteous" (1 Jn. 2:1).

The Epistle to the Hebrews portrays intercession through the cultic imagery of priesthood. A priest is one who works on behalf of others. According to this epistle, Jesus Christ "does not have to work on his own behalf and is therefore free to work on behalf of those whom he does not feel ashamed to call brothers. He does the works of another. Jesus does 'the works of the Father,' as John's Gospel says and reports him to have said. But he also does the works of man, standing as the One for many."[45] Thus the Christology of the epistle is at once high and human. It is high—for the Son is "the effulgence of God's splendour and the stamp of God's very being" (Heb. 1:3, NEB). It is human—for this Son "is not ashamed to call them brethren" (2:11) and "himself likewise partook of the same nature, . . . made like his brethren in every respect, so that he might become a merciful and faithful high priest in the service of God. . . . For because he himself has suffered and been tempted, he is able to help those who are tempted" (2:14,17–18). Through his entrance into the Holy "he is able for all time to save those who draw near to God through him, since he always lives to make intercession for them" (7:25). "For Christ has entered . . . into heaven itself, now to appear in the presence of God on our behalf" (9:24). That is how Christ is "the pioneer and perfector of our faith" (12:2). In its own way this theology is analogous to the Johannine portrayal of Christ as "the way." The continuing work of Jesus Christ is possible because through the resurrection and ascension "the man for others" will always have God's ear.

Easter as God's Victory

Another image that the New Testament employs to portray the resurrection as God's saving act is that of victorious
struggle. This imagery is kingly rather than priestly, military
rather than sacerdotal. If the conflict with demons marks the
Synoptic portrayal of the ministry of Jesus, his resurrection
manifests the ultimate defeat of the powers of evil.

The Easter narratives portray "Christus Victor." In all
four Gospels the stone has been rolled away from the tomb.
Albert Camus has pointed us to the contemporary significance of the ancient myth of Sisyphus, condemned forever to
roll a great stone up a mountain only to have it elude his
grasp.[46] Gerhard Gloege saw the myth's reversal in the gospel
of the resurrection. "The Gospel of Jesus of Nazareth declares that Sisyphus has already been rescued from himself.
It happened at Easter. The stone has been rolled away (Mk.
16:4) by the invisible hand of a stranger. It was not Jesus who
rolled it away. Someone else rolled it away for Jesus. This
someone has also rolled it away for Sisyphus—once and for
all."[47] The stone that was too much for Sisyphus was not too
much for God.

Paul links the image of triumph with others in Col. 2:
13–15: "God made [us] alive together with him, having forgiven us all our trespasses, having canceled the bond which
stood against us with its legal demands; this he set aside,
nailing it to the cross. He disarmed the principalities and
powers and made a public example of them, triumphing over
them in him." [RSV reads *en autō* as masculine, "in him,"
while NEB renders it as neuter, "in it" ("On that cross he
discarded the cosmic powers and authorities like a garment;
he made a public spectacle of them and led them as captives
in his triumphal procession").] That is to say, instead of the
cross being the defeat of righteousness, it is God's victory
through the resurrection. For Paul, "the rulers of this age"
who did not understand what they were doing when they
crucified the Lord of glory (1 Cor. 2:8) are not the Jewish

authorities who acted in ignorance (cf. Acts 3:17) but the principalities and powers whose dominion has been over-come in the cross and resurrection.

Again, for Paul, death is the last enemy which shall be overthrown because death has been conquered in principle at Easter. " 'O death, where is thy victory? O death, where is thy sting?' . . . Thanks be to God, who gives us the victory through our Lord Jesus Christ" (1 Cor. 15:55, 57). That is why Paul is confident that "neither death, nor life, nor angels, nor principalities, nor things present, nor things to come, nor powers, nor height, nor depth, nor anything else in all crea-tion, will be able to separate us from the love of God in Christ Jesus our Lord" (Rom. 8:38–39).

The imagery of victorious struggle is evident in the Johan-nine theology. The hour of the passion is also the hour of the glory. As that hour approaches, Jesus says, "Now is the judgment of this world, now shall the ruler of this world be cast out" (Jn. 12:31). To his followers on that last night Jesus says, "In the world you have tribulation; but be of good cheer, I have overcome the world" (16:33). Little wonder that in this Gospel the last word from the cross is not a prayer but a victor's shout: "It is finished" (19:30).

The First Epistle of Peter puts this imagery of victorious conquest in such fashion as to suggest that there is no nook or cranny in all creation where the victorious word of the gospel has not penetrated: "being put to death in the flesh but made alive in the spirit; in which he went and preached to the spirits in prison" (1 Pet. 3:18–19).[48]

As we would expect, the imagery of triumph is dominant in the Apocalypse. It is because Christ is the one who died and is alive forever that he has the keys of Death and Hades (Rev. 1:18). The slain Lamb is "the Lion of the tribe of Judah, the Root of David" who *has conquered* (5:5).

Our liturgies and hymnody abound in this praise of Christ as Victor:

> The strife is o'er, the battle done;
> The victory of life is won;
> The song of triumph has begun. Alleluia!
>
> The powers of death have done their worst,
> But Christ their legions hath dispersed:
> Let shouts of holy joy outburst. Alleluia![49]

The Christus Victor theme has been woven into the theology and poetry of Easter faith, sometimes employing images of combat not employed in the New Testament. An example is George Herbert:

> The rest of our Creation
> Our great Redeemer did remove
> With the same shake, which at his passion
> Did th'earth and all things with it move.
> As Samson bore the doores away,
> Christs hands, though nail'd, wrought our salvation,
> And did unhinge that day.[50]

The New Testament heralds the resurrection as God's victory of love over death and darkness. What makes this imagery relevant for apostolic faith is the confidence that this victory was won for us. God "has delivered us from the dominion of darkness" (Col. 1:13). Even those faltering Christians of Laodicea were invited to sit with Christ on his throne as he himself conquered and sat with the Father on his throne (Rev. 3:21).

Easter, the Church and Its Mission

As the resurrection of Jesus has a once-for-all character, so the message of the resurrection was entrusted to a unique body of messengers. Of course, what happened at Easter continued and fulfilled what was begun in the ministry of Jesus. Jesus of Nazareth had called the Twelve and sent them to proclaim in word and deed that the kingdom of God was at hand. In that sense the apostolic church *in nuce* goes back to the pre-Easter ministry of Jesus. Nonetheless, it was Easter that constituted the church and validated its mission.

Here a word needs to be said about the list of witnesses to which Paul appeals in 1 Cor. 15:3–8 (Peter, the Twelve, the five hundred, James, all the apostles, Paul himself). Some scholars, notably Ulrich Wilckens,[51] have suggested that the primary purpose of the Easter appearances was not to attest the reality of the resurrection but to attest and "legitimate" the messengers—to attest their authority. If these verses are "legitimation formulas," the frame of reference is really that of church order. However, so to stress the "legitimation" of the messengers does less than justice to Paul's purpose. It is hardly likely that the appearance to an unnamed five hundred people can be understood in this manner.[52] The literary style of the early creed indicates that the appearances to Peter and to the Twelve are part of the message itself.

Although we cannot interpret the whole purpose of the appearances as a legitimation of church authority, we must not overlook the element of truth in this view. "Whether then it was I or they, so we preach and so you believed" (1 Cor. 15:11). Paul affirms his own apostolic credentials: "For I am the least of the apostles, unfit to be called an apostle. . . . But by the grace of God I am what I am" (15:9–10). Similarly, in 1 Cor. 9:1, he appeals to his encounter with the risen Lord as his credential: "Am I not an apostle? Have I not seen Jesus our Lord?"

Whether or not we distinguish appearances that are consitutive for the founding of the church from those that are more functional as "mission inaugurating" and "mission validating,"[53] we recognize in the early formulas a declaration that God began something new when he raised Jesus from the dead—God constituted the church and validated its mission.

Luke expresses a similar concern but in somewhat different fashion. The circle of the Twelve, broken by Judas' betrayal, must be reconstituted by the Lord. Matthias was one who "accompanied us during all the time that the Lord Jesus went in and out among us, beginning from the baptism of John until the day when he was taken up from us" and so he becomes "with us a witness to his resurrection" (Acts 1: 21–22).

Luke's conception of apostleship is not identical with Paul's, for Luke equates the apostles with the Twelve. Already in his first volume we read that Jesus "called his disciples, and chose from them twelve, whom he named apostles" (Lk. 6:13). That company of twelve apostles is reconstituted through the appointment of Matthias. Characteristically, Luke's Paul says, "God raised him [Jesus] from the dead; and for many days he appeared to those who came up with him from Galilee to Jerusalem, who are now his witnesses to the people" (Acts 13:30–31). Luke's Paul does not speak of his own encounter with the risen Lord as though this constituted a resurrection appearance, for in Luke's view those appearances terminated with the ascension. This is in marked contrast to Paul's own words in 1 Cor. 15:8.

In his letters Paul does not limit apostleship in this manner. Andronicus and Junias are not only his kinsmen and fellow prisoners but "men of note among the apostles" (Rom. 16:7). While it is possible to interpret this phrase to mean that these two were persons of note in the eyes of the apostles, it is more probable that Paul refers to these two as themselves apostles. Similarly, we may assume that Paul's statement that Christ appeared "to all the apostles" (1 Cor. 15:7) is not a repetition of the preceding statement that Christ appeared "to the twelve" but rather refers to another and larger group of witnesses. Paul may say that he is "unfit to be called an apostle" but he never doubts that his apostleship has been validated directly by the risen Lord. He knows himself to be "called to be an apostle" (Rom. 1:1; 1 Cor. 1:1; etc.). His apostleship is "not from men nor through man, but through Jesus Christ and God the Father, who raised him from the dead" (Gal. 1:1). God "was pleased to reveal his Son to me, in order that I might preach him among the Gentiles" (Gal. 1:16). When Paul visited Jerusalem he "saw none of the other apostles except James the Lord's brother" (Gal. 1:19). Luke gives James a prominent place in the Jerusalem church but does not call him an apostle.

And yet, we must not exaggerate the differences between Paul and Luke on the meaning of apostleship.[54] For both, apostleship rests on a unique encounter with the risen Lord. Unquestionably, Luke equated the apostles with the Twelve at the outset of the church's mission in a way that Paul does not. But does that mean that Luke could envision no addition to the apostolic company? In Acts 14:4,14, Luke calls Paul and Barnabas apostles. Did Luke here take over some traditions absentmindedly—or have we tried to deduce more from Luke's stress on the original constitution of the Twelve than the evidence merits? R. H. Fuller goes beyond the evidence when he says that the basic tendency of Luke's portrayal of Paul in Acts is "to downgrade him" as one who stands in the apostolic succession but who is not himself an apostle.[55] In Luke's three accounts of Paul's encounter with Christ on the Damascus road (Acts 9; 22; and 26) the vision *(optasia)* is far more than a conversion experience. It is Christ's call to mission. Ian H. Marshall suggests that the basic difference in Luke's resurrection appearances to the Twelve lies in that they were validated for the mission to Israel (cf. Acts 13: 24,31), while Paul's "post-resurrection" encounter sent him to the Gentiles (Acts 9:15; 22:21; 26:17). After all, that is the path of the Christian mission in Acts—first to Israel and then to the Gentiles. This is consistent with Luke's own Easter witness "that in his name repentance bringing the forgiveness of sins is to be proclaimed to all nations. Begin from Jerusalem; it is you [the Twelve] who are witnesses to it all" (Lk. 24:47–48, NEB; cf. Acts 1:8).

In any case, all the Evangelists interpret the resurrection appearances as validating the church's mission. What is still a promise in Mark ("But go, tell his disciples and Peter that he is going before you to Galilee," Mk. 16:7) is seen fulfilled in Matthew: "Now the eleven disciples went to Galilee, to the mountain to which Jesus had directed them" (Mt. 28:16).

There they hear him say, "Go therefore and make disciples of all nations, baptizing them, . . . teaching them to observe all that I have commanded you" (Mt. 28:19–20). In John the call to mission is also evident: "As the Father has sent me, even so I send you" (20:21), thus fulfilling Jesus' prayer "for those who believe in me through their word" (17:20).

In various ways the New Testament affirms that Easter constituted the church and entrusted to chosen messengers the good news of the resurrection. It was not because these first witnesses were superior folk but because they had been chosen by God to participate in the saving work of God that they became pillars and foundation stones of the ongoing mission. Their part in the story of salvation is unrepeatable and is constitutive for all later activity. Their part in the story is analogous to the place of the patriarchs in Old Testament story.

Easter, the Spirit, and the End Time

Something more needs to be said. At Easter, God constituted the church and its mission—not only by validating an apostolate but by bestowing the Spirit as the guarantee of the new age.

We shall defer until a later chapter a discussion of the relationship between Lord and Spirit. Here it is enough to call attention to Pentecost as a decisive event in the past which is inseparably linked with the Easter time.

The Fourth Gospel emphasizes this relationship by placing the gift of the Spirit on Easter evening. "Jesus said to them again, 'Peace be with you. As the Father has sent me, even so I send you.' And when he had said this, he breathed on them, and said to them, 'Receive the Holy Spirit' " (Jn. 20:21–22). According to Luke, the risen Lord promised the Spirit at Easter (Lk. 24:49; cf. Acts 1:5,8) and, as the ascended Lord, he bestowed the Spirit from heaven at Pentecost. In Peter's words, "Being therefore exalted at the right hand of God, and having received from the Father the promise of the Holy Spirit, he has poured out this which you see and hear" (Acts 2:33).

In the Old Testament the Spirit of God is the Spirit of power and of prophecy. But rabbinic Judaism held that the Spirit of prophecy had departed from Israel after the last prophets.[56] Israel's faith looked forward to a new day. Then the Messiah would appear as one endowed with the Holy Spirit (e.g., Isa. 11:2). Indeed, the last days would see a powerful return of the Spirit of prophecy beyond any expression in the past.

> And it shall come to pass afterward,
> that I will pour out my spirit on all flesh;
> your sons and your daughters shall prophesy,
> your old men shall dream dreams,
> and your young men shall see visions.
> Even upon the menservants and maidservants
> in those days, I will pour out my spirit.
> (Joel 2:28–29)

When Peter was asked what was happening at Pentecost, he replied that "this is what was spoken by the prophet Joel" (Acts 2:16). With the resurrection and exaltation of Jesus, the new age has dawned. Jesus, the bearer of the Spirit, has become the giver of the Spirit. Paul can call the risen Lord "a life-giving spirit" (1 Cor. 15:45). Christians are those "upon whom the end of the ages has come" (1 Cor. 10:11).

The New Testament gives frequent and varied expression to this central conviction that with the cross and resurrection the new age has been inaugurated.

It is not accidental that in the Synoptic Gospels the apocalyptic discourse about the close of the age (Matthew 24 to 25; Mark 13; Luke 21) immediately precedes the passion and resurrection.[57] Especially in Matthew, the motifs that shape the vision of the future all recur in what follows. Jesus speaks of betrayal and of many falling away (Mt. 24:10f.)—and soon he is betrayed while his disciples fall away. Jesus warns, "Watch therefore" (24:42)—and he will say it again in Gethsemane. Jesus speaks of a great tribulation coming (24: 9,21)—and soon he himself must undergo it. Jesus speaks of cosmic signs attending the end—earthquake (24:7), the sun darkened (24:29)—and at the hour of his death the sun was darkened while the earth shook, and at Easter there is another earthquake (28:2). Then, Jesus says, after all these convulsive signs the Son of Man will appear in glory (24:30) —and Matthew's Easter chapter closes with an appearing that reflects Daniel's vision of the Son of Man who receives power and authority. Perhaps this is the way to understand Jesus' word that "this generation will not pass away till all these things take place" (24:34).

In this context we may place Matthew's description of Jesus' death—when "the earth shook, and the rocks were split; the tombs also were opened, and many bodies of the saints who had fallen asleep were raised, and coming out of the tombs after his resurrection they went into the holy city and appeared to many" (27:51–53). Matthew can place this apocalyptic portrayal of the future in the heart of his passion narrative because he looks at the cross from its resurrection side.

To see the cross and resurrection as the inauguration of the end time is not confined to apocalyptic tradition. The Fourth Gospel has its own characteristic way of seeing the future already evidenced in the life of Jesus. "Truly, truly, I say to you, the hour is coming, and now is, when the dead will hear the voice of the Son of God, and those who hear will live" (Jn. 5:25). This is followed immediately[58] by a reference to the traditional last day: "The hour is coming when all who are in the tombs will hear his voice and come forth" (5:28; cf. 6:40). Later, when Martha speaks of the last day, Jesus replies, "I am the resurrection and the life; he who believes in me, though he die, yet shall he live, and whoever lives and believes in me shall never die" (11:25–26).

If there is a "not yet," there is also a "no longer." The new world has dawned in the resurrection of Jesus. Paul expresses the "no longer" in memorable lines: "And he died for all, that those who live might live no longer for themselves but for him who for their sake died and was raised" (2 Cor. 5:15). That is why Paul sometimes puts the whole of God's saving purpose in the aorist past tense: "For those whom he foreknew he also predestined to be conformed to the image of his Son, in order that he might be the first-born among many brethren. And those whom he predestined he also called; and those whom he called he also justified; and those whom he justified he also glorified" (Rom. 8:29–30). It was not merely literary style that led Paul to place the verb "glorified" in the same tense as the preceding verbs. The end time is the time of salvation—and salvation has come in the resurrection of Jesus.

Throughout this chapter we have seen how the past and present and future dimensions of Easter's meaning are interrelated. The last section—that Easter has inaugurated the end time—leads us in the following chapter to examine how Easter discloses the future.

But Easter began as a given past. The New Testament message does not allow us to make of the resurrection of Jesus a timeless symbol. It bears witness to the historical reality of the resurrection. New Testament faith confesses that in a particular past, the history of Jesus of Nazareth, God has acted decisively by raising him from the dead. That past ensures the future and governs the present. Because Easter has its own time and place it can touch every time and every place.

APPENDIX TO CHAPTER II

PSALMS, PASSION NARRATIVE, AND EMPTY GRAVE[1]

A QUESTION

The creed in 1 Cor. 15:3 affirms "that Christ died for our sins in accordance with the scriptures." What Scriptures? New Testament writers turn to various Scriptures to interpret the mystery and meaning of the cross. A familiar example is the use of Isaiah 53 (cf. Acts 8:32f.). But where does the passion narrative (Mark 14 to 15) turn?

The Evangelist offers us a clue. Just before Jesus died, we read, he cried with a loud voice, "My God, my God, why hast thou forsaken me?" (Mk. 15:34). That cry is a quotation from Ps. 22. This is one of a group of psalms in which the righteous sufferer cries out to God for vindication. The question of the psalmist is also the question raised by the crucifixion. Has God forsaken his righteous servant? Think of it! God's righteous one, delivered into the hands of sinners (Mk. 14:41)!

The cry of dereliction does not stand alone. Let us follow Mark's narrative and see how often these psalms are directly cited or strongly suggested.

THE PLOT

Mark's narrative of the passion begins in 14:1. "And the chief priests and the scribes were seeking how to arrest him by stealth, and kill him."

Ps. 37:32   The wicked watches the righteous,
and seeks to slay him.

Ps. 54:3   For insolent men have risen against me,
ruthless men seek my life.

Ps. 86:14   O God, insolent men have risen up against me;
a band of ruthless men seek my life.

THE BETRAYAL FORETOLD

At the supper Jesus says, "Truly, I say to you, one of you will betray me, one who is eating with me. . . . For the Son of man goes as it is written of him, but woe to that man by whom the Son of man is betrayed!" (Mk. 14:17,21).

Ps. 41:9   Even my bosom friend in whom I trusted,
                    who ate of my bread, has lifted his heel
                    against me.
            (Jn. 13:18 cites this quotation.)

Ps. 55:12–14   It is not an enemy who taunts me—
                        then I could bear it;
                    it is not an adversary who deals insolently
                            with me—
                        then I could hide from him.
                    But it is you, my equal,
                        my companion, my familiar friend.
                    We used to hold sweet converse together;
                        within God's house we walked in fellowship.
                    (Rabbinic commentary associated this psalm
                    with Ahithophel, who betrayed David and
                    hanged himself. Compare 2 Sam. 17:23 with
                    Mt. 27:5.)[2]

GETHSEMANE

"And they went to a place which was called Gethsemane. . . . And he said to them, 'My soul is very sorrowful, even to death.' " (Mk. 14:32,34)

Ps. 55:4–5   My heart is in anguish within me,
                    the terrors of death have fallen upon me.
                Fear and trembling come upon me,
                    and horror overwhelms me.

DISCIPLES FLEE

At the arrest of Jesus we read, "And they all forsook him, and fled" (Mk. 14:50).

Ps. 38:11   My friends and companions stand aloof
                        from my plague,
                     and my kinsmen stand afar off.

FALSE WITNESSES

At the trial of Jesus "many bore false witness against him, and their witness did not agree" (Mk. 14:56).

Ps. 27:12   For false witnesses have risen against me,
                     and they breathe out violence.

Ps. 35:11   Malicious witnesses rise up;
                     they ask me of things that I know not.

Ps. 109:1–5   Be not silent, O God of my praise!
                     For wicked and deceitful mouths are opened
                        against me,
                        speaking against me with lying tongues.
                     They beset me with words of hate,
                        and attack me without cause.
                     In return for my love they accuse me,
                        even as I make prayer for them.
                     So they reward me evil for good,
                        and hatred for my love.

THE SILENCE OF JESUS

"And the high priest stood up in the midst, and asked Jesus, 'Have you no answer to make? What is it that these men testify against you?' But he was silent and made no answer" (Mk. 14:60–61).

Ps. 38:12–14   Those who seek my life lay their snares,
                        those who seek my hurt speak of ruin,
                        and meditate treachery all the day long.
                     But I am like a deaf man, I do not hear,
                        like a dumb man who does not open his
                           mouth.
                     Yea, I am like a man who does not hear,
                        and in whose mouth are no rebukes.

Ps. 39:9   I am dumb, I do not open my mouth.
(Here we may also think of Isa. 53:7, "He was
afflicted, yet he opened not his mouth." But
it is the psalms that shape the passion
narrative.)

THE CRUCIFIXION

"And they crucified him, and divided his garments among them,
casting lots for them, to decide what each should take" (Mk. 15:24).

Ps. 22:18   They divide my garments among them,
and for my raiment they cast lots.
(Jn. 19:24 says, "This was to fulfil the
scripture.")

THE MOCKING

"And those who passed by derided him, wagging their heads, and
saying, 'Aha! You who would destroy the temple . . . save yourself!'"
(Mk. 15:29).

Ps. 35:21   They open wide their mouths against me;
they say, 'Aha, Aha!
our eyes have seen it!'

Ps. 109:25   I am an object of scorn to my accusers;
when they see me, they wag their heads.

THE CRY

"And at the ninth hour Jesus cried with a loud voice, 'Eloi, Eloi,
lama sabachthani?' which means, 'My God, my God, why hast thou
forsaken me?' " (Mk. 15:34).

Ps. 22:1   My God, my God, why hast thou forsaken me?
Why art thou so far from helping me,
from the words of my groaning?

THE VINEGAR

"And one ran and, filling a sponge full of vinegar, put it on a reed and gave it to him to drink" (Mk. 15:36).

> Ps. 69:21   They gave me poison for food,
> and for my thirst they gave me vinegar to
> drink.

WHAT DOES ALL THIS MEAN?

These psalms were not written as predictions of Jesus. They were wrung from the hearts of faithful Jews who in their distress cried out to God for vindication. Their cries were undergirded and answered by an unshakable trust in the God who delivers. We must not take these psalms away from those who first uttered them.

Nor do they fit Jesus in every instance. The psalmist knows that he shares in human guilt: "I am sorry for my sin" (Ps. 38:18). This is not Jesus "who in every respect has been tempted as we are, yet without sin" (Heb. 4:15).

Moreover, the psalmist wants God to avenge him:

> He will requite my enemies with evil;
> in thy faithfulness put an end to them. (Ps. 54:5)

> Let death come upon them;
> let them go down to Sheol alive;
> let them go away in terror into their graves. (Ps. 55:15)

Again, this is not Jesus who prays, "Father, forgive them; for they know not what they do" (Lk. 23:34).

If these psalms are not predictions, how do they serve to shape the passion narrative of the gospel? How is the death of Jesus "in accordance with the scriptures"? The Evangelist sees faithful Israel embodied in Jesus, Israel's suffering incarnated in Jesus, and Israel's hope fulfilled in Jesus.

IS THIS ALL?

Does the Evangelist think only of isolated verses from these psalms —or does he appropriate them as a whole?

These psalms not only render the sufferer's cry to God; each of them ends with assurance and praise. For example, Ps. 22 alternates between despair and assurance—and it ends with praise. Notice how Heb. 2:12 uses Ps. 22:22. Would Mark do less?

After all, the question of God's vindication in the psalms is also the question of the passion narrative. Has God forsaken his righteous one? Surely not! The story of the cross could not be at the heart of early Christian worship and witness were that so.

Before turning to Mark's answer, let us return to those psalms we have cited to see how each of them moves from lament to assurance and praise.

Ps. 22:24 For he has not despised or abhorred
        the affliction of the afflicted;
    and he has not hid his face from him,
        but has heard, when he cried to him.

Ps. 35:9 Then my soul shall rejoice in the Lord,
        exulting in his deliverance.

Ps. 37:32–33 The wicked watches the righteous,
        and seeks to slay him.
    The Lord will not abandon him to his power.

Ps. 38:15 But for thee, O Lord, do I wait;
        it is thou, O Lord my God, who wilt answer.

Ps. 39:7 And now, Lord, for what do I wait?
        My hope is in thee.

Ps. 41:12 But thou hast upheld me because of my integrity,
        and set me in thy presence forever.

Ps. 54:4 Behold, God is my helper;
        the Lord is the upholder of my life.

Ps. 55:16 But I call upon God;
        and the Lord will save me.

Ps. 69:9,13 For zeal for thy house has consumed me. . . .
    But as for me, my prayer is to thee, O Lord.
      At an acceptable time, O God,
        in the abundance of thy steadfast love
          answer me.

> (Jn. 2:17 links the first line of this quotation
> with Jesus' cleansing of the Temple as this is
> remembered by Easter faith.)

Ps. 86:7   In the day of my trouble I call on thee,
> for thou dost answer me.

Ps. 109:30–31   With my mouth I will give great thanks to
> the Lord;
> I will praise him in the midst of the
> throng.
> For he stands at the right hand of the
> needy,
> to save him from those who condemn him
> to death.

GOD HAS NOT FORSAKEN HIS RIGHTEOUS ONE

If these psalms do not end in despair but in hope and praise, can the passion narrative do less? Mark's narrative does not end with the burial of Jesus, but with the empty grave. "Do not be amazed; you seek Jesus of Nazareth, who was crucified. He has risen, he is not here; see the place where they laid him" (Mk. 16:6). God has not left him where they laid him.

CONCLUSION

In one of his letters, Paul writes: "We preach Christ crucified, a stumbling block to Jews and folly to Gentiles, but to those who are called, both Jews and Greeks, Christ the power of God and the wisdom of God" (1 Cor. 1:23–24). That is to say, the gospel of the cross is God's *new* word and deed.

Yet the God who reveals the far reach of his love in the cross is the God of Israel. That is why the early creed says "that Christ died for our sins in accordance with the scriptures." That is the way in which Mark's narrative is written—according to the Scriptures, according to the psalms of the righteous. This does not mean that the story of the cross is simply created out of these Old Testament texts. Nothing is more sure than that Jesus died on a cross. Nor is there reason to doubt that he, whose whole ministry was imbued with God's will as he knew this from Scripture, should intuitively and spontaneously make the psalmist's cry his own. In his death as in his life Jesus expressed his utter solidarity with Israel.

But the story of the cross is gospel—and that good news is more than historical report but is told "in accordance with the scriptures." How else would we expect it to be told? Disciples, we know, had fled. The death and resurrection of Jesus sent his followers back to their Bible. They discovered that "all the promises of God find their Yes in him" (2 Cor. 1:20).

We can be grateful that this is so. These psalms, with their question, remind us that the cross is a mystery. All the biblical images that portray Christ's death for our sins, and all the doctrines of the atonement, cannot dispel the mystery of God's love.

We sense this in the cry that Jesus made his own: "My God, my God, why hast thou forsaken me?" The words reveal a mystery and present in mystery a revelation. G. Campbell Morgan, a biblical expositor of yesteryear, once said that whenever anyone asked him for a theory of the atonement he could only reply that, if the Lord himself asked "Why?" he would not presume to explain the mystery of his pain.[3]

A familiar passion chorale makes the same reminder:

> What language shall I borrow
> To thank thee, dearest Friend,
> For this thy dying sorrow,
> Thy pity without end?

What language indeed. The Evangelist incorporates the language of Israel's memory and hope. The psalmist's questions are ringed with exclamation points of trust and praise. So is the question in the passion narrative. "He has risen, he is not here." God has not forsaken him.

III

The Resurrection
as Disclosure
of the Future

Memory and hope are joined in the New Testament message of the resurrection. Easter speaks of a "not yet" as well as of a "no longer." Our attention has been drawn to texts in which the future is seen as having dawned in what happened at Easter. "The last day" is already manifest in "the third day."

At the Last Supper Jesus had said, "Truly, I say to you, I shall not drink again of the fruit of the vine until that day when I drink it new in the kingdom of God" (Mk. 14:25; cf. Mt. 26:29; Lk. 22:18). "That day" is "the last day"—but this last day is anticipated and assured in the new fellowship. In Luke's Emmaus narrative the risen Lord was known in the breaking of bread (Lk. 24:30,35). Peter tells Cornelius that "God raised him [Jesus] on the third day and made him manifest; not to all the people but to us who were chosen by God as witnesses, who ate and drank with him after he rose from the dead" (Acts 10:40–41). Memory and hope are joined in the Pauline tradition of the Supper. The Supper points back to the night in which the Lord was delivered up; it points forward as well. "For as often as you eat this bread and drink the cup, you proclaim the Lord's death until he comes" (1 Cor. 11:26).

Christians are those "upon whom the end of the ages has come" (1 Cor. 10:11). Such an overwhelming conviction that the future has broken into the present had its dangers. It could lead to impatience instead of to mission. "Lord, will you at this time restore the kingdom to Israel?" (Acts 1:6). That is why Luke's narrative of the ascension serves as "an eschatological pause"[1] which sends Jesus' followers into the world to do his will. Disciples will not reach the future by speculating about "times and seasons" or by "gazing into heaven." They are given marching orders, not blueprints of the future.

Enthusiasm could lead to worse dangers. Why did Paul's readers in Corinth deny the resurrection of the dead if they could affirm the resurrection of Jesus? Apparently, Corinthian enthusiasm was so confident of present arrival that it needed no future. "Already you are filled! Already you have become rich!" (1 Cor. 4:8). The presumptions of such enthusiasm are clearly discernible in 1 Corinthians 12 to 14 and in 2 Corinthians 11 to 12. Paul had to counter this "triumphalism" with the "not yet" of apocalyptic eschatology (1 Corinthians 15) and with his message of the cross. The latter finds its most eloquent expression in Paul's own testimony: "that I may know him and the power of his resurrection, and may share his sufferings, becoming like him in his death, that if possible I may attain the resurrection from the dead" (Phil. 3:10–11). The dawning of the new age does not dispense with the "not yet" of what will be. Paul warns against those who say "that the [future] day of the Lord has come" (2 Thess. 2:1). Similarly, the pastoral epistles rebuke Hymenaeus and Philetus "who have swerved from the truth by holding that the [future] resurrection is past already" (2 Tim. 2:18). Such warnings are consistent with Jesus' warnings that "the end is not yet" (Mk. 13:7 and parallels).

Much has been written about the effect which the delay of Christ's final coming *(parousia)* had on the early church. More attention needs to be given to the danger posed by the illusion of final arrival. Against all such illusions the New Testament insists that Easter and the gift of the Spirit were but the earnest, the guarantee *(arrabōn),* of what will be.

Still, misunderstanding bears its own witness to the conviction that the resurrection of Jesus Christ has ushered in the new world of the future. "But in fact Christ has been raised from the dead, the first fruits of those who have fallen asleep" (1 Cor. 15:20).

Paul Minear wrote a helpful volume for the Evanston Assembly of the World Council of Churches (1954). The theme of that Assembly was "Christ the Hope of the World." Minear suggested some New Testament reminders that are relevant to our present discussion:[2]

— In the Bible the ground of hope is always personal. The Old Testament's "hope in God" finds expression in the New Testament as "Christ in you, the hope of glory."
— In the Bible hope is always singular. A person cannot really live by more than one hope.
— Hope springs from what God has done and is doing, not from the notion that he might do something else. For that reason, hope is not the opposite of memory, for memory can apply to the future just as hope can apply to the past. "In this hope we *were* saved."[3]
— Hope is nondetachable. The old adage, "While there's life, there's hope" is reversed. Without hope there is no real life.

Hope is based on what God has done. Christians are those who "have been born anew to a living hope through the resurrection of Jesus Christ from the dead" (1 Pet. 1:3).

The significance of the resurrection of Jesus for the future is the central concern of 1 Corinthians 15. "Now if Christ is preached as raised from the dead, how can some of you say that there is no resurrection of the dead?" (v. 12). The Christ who has been raised is the firstfruits. Elsewhere Paul says, "For since we believe that Jesus died and rose again, even so, through Jesus, God will bring with him those who have fallen asleep" (1 Thess. 4:14). That is why "we await a Savior, the Lord Jesus Christ, who will change our lowly body to be like his glorious body" (Phil. 3:20–21).

Easter means both memory and hope. Mary Magdalene

must not try to cling to the past as though Easter is simply a return to the past. "Do not hold me, for I have not yet ascended to the Father" (Jn. 20:17). Mary needed the "forward" look. But Thomas needed to be sure that the Lord of the future is the Jesus he had known. "Put your finger here, and see my hands; and put out your hand, and place it in my side" (20:27).

Luke's ascension imagery should not be identified with that of John, but his last scene carries a similar reminder that Easter time points forward: "This Jesus, who was taken up from you into heaven, will come in the same way as you saw him go into heaven" (Acts 1:11). And Matthew's last scene has its own reminder of the future—"to the close of the age."

With these preliminary observations we turn to the New Testament message to see how the resurrection of Jesus is the disclosure of the future.

EASTER REVEALS THE FUTURE
OF JESUS CHRIST

This is surely the place to begin—not with our future but with his.

MEMORY AND HOPE

We have noted earlier how the apocalyptic discourse in the Synoptic Gospels is linked integrally with the narratives of Jesus' passion and resurrection. In the same way, the vision of the future in the Apocalypse is linked with the central saving event of the cross and resurrection. The Lion of the tribe of Judah who has conquered and is able to open the seven seals of the future is and will always be the Lamb who was slain. Jacques Ellul[4] suggests that the whole structure of the Apocalypse finds its key in the central importance of chs. 11 and 12 which portray in apocalyptic colors the significance of the incarnation, cross, and resurrection. As he notes, in pagan mythology what happens on earth is deter-

mined by what happens in heaven—where friendly or hostile
deities determine what happens to a Ulysses or an Aeneas.
In biblical apocalyptic, what happened on earth determines
what happens in heaven. The "war in heaven" (Rev. 12:7) is
preceded by the gospel of the incarnation—for the woman
gives birth to the child who is caught up to God and his
throne (12:5). That child is the Lord who was crucified (11:
8). That is to say, the struggle that occurred on earth is the
key to the cosmic struggle. God's victory on earth is the key
to his ultimate victory in Christ. Biblical apocalypse is not
flight from the world or wishful thinking.

Memory and hope are continually intersecting in John's
vision of the future. If the Apocalypse begins with a promise
("Behold, I am coming soon") and if it closes with a prayer
("Even so, come, Lord Jesus"), all the way through the book
—and long before we come to the final vision of a new heaven
and earth—hope is intersected by the jubilant hymnody of
memory. The King of kings and Lord of lords, who leads the
armies of heaven to the final overthrow of evil, is the rider
on the white horse, clad in a robe dipped in blood (Rev.
19:11ff.). But his robe is dipped in blood before he rides into
the final battle. Thus it must be his own blood,[5] once shed on
the cross. Always memory and hope intersect in this
strangely magnificent panorama. The Hallelujah Chorus precedes the final curtain. Even while praying "Come, Lord
Jesus," John has heard the voice from the throne say, "It is
done!"

We know that for many Christians the book of Revelation
is a puzzle and a problem. Not a few have been repulsed by
its lurid and violent images. The Muratorian Canon list from
the late second century indicates that this has been so from
the early days of the church. "We have included the Revelations of John and of Peter, although some of us will not let
them be read in church."[6] During a time when many apoca-
lypses were written, these two were most prominent. Why
did John's Apocalypse find its way into the canon of the New
Testament while that of Peter did not? This is not simply due

to the fact that our book of Revelation is a first-century document which tradition associated with the apostle John, while the other is later. The latter is primarily absorbed with the future of saints and sinners—and especially with the final judgment of sinners in colors that have left their mark on our art and literature. For all the difficulties we may have with John's Apocalypse, its central concern is with the future of Jesus Christ expressed in the recurring doxologies and hymnody of worship.[7] That is an important difference. The book bears its own characteristic and eloquent witness to the confession that the risen Jesus Christ is Lord.

GLORY

Easter is the revelation of the glory of God, a glory which has been revealed and will be revealed in Jesus Christ.

When we examined the language of the resurrection we noted how often the verb "appeared" *(ōphthē)* calls to mind the Old Testament theophanies. Stephen's words, "The God of glory appeared to our father Abraham" (Acts 7:2), call to mind a number of occasions when the Greek Old Testament uses *ōphthē* in precisely this manner ("The glory of the Lord appeared" in Ex. 16:10; Num. 14:10; 16:19, 42; 20:6). God is the God of glory. His coming is the appearing of his glory.

For New Testament faith this glory is revealed in Jesus Christ. Stephen "gazed into heaven and saw the glory of God, and Jesus standing at the right hand of God" (Acts 7:55). Luke had portrayed the birth of Jesus as manifesting the glory of God. "And an angel of the Lord appeared to them [the shepherds], and the glory of the Lord shone around them. . . . And suddenly there was with the angel a multitude of the heavenly host praising God and saying, 'Glory to God in the highest . . .' " (Lk. 2:9, 13–14). Little wonder that "the shepherds returned, glorifying and praising God for all that they had heard and seen" (2:20). The incarnation is the coming of the glory of God. So too the Johannine prologue exults: "And the Word became flesh and dwelt among us, full of grace and truth; we have beheld his glory, glory as of the only Son from the Father" (Jn. 1:14).

God's glory was seen in the ministry of Jesus. In the Synoptic Gospels it breaks through especially in the transfiguration of Jesus. Luke says that Moses and Elijah "appeared in glory" to speak with Jesus about his exodus which he was to accomplish in Jerusalem (Lk. 9:30–31). We read that "a cloud came and overshadowed them; and they were afraid as they entered the cloud. And a voice came out of the cloud, saying, 'This is my Son, my Chosen; listen to him!' " (Lk. 9:34–35). The "cloud" in Scripture is the biblical image for "the elusive presence" of God's glory (cf. Ex. 16:10; 19:9; 24:15f.; Num. 14:10; etc.). While some scholars have suggested that the transfiguration is a misplaced resurrection story, it lacks the characteristic features of these appearances.[8] It is best to interpret the transfiguration story as a promise and an anticipation of the disclosure of Christ's glory at Easter and at the end. When the Second Epistle of Peter seeks to validate the apostolic testimony, it does so with reference to the transfiguration scene: "We were eyewitnesses of his majesty. For when he received honor and glory from God the Father and the voice was borne to him by the Majestic Glory . . . we heard this voice borne from heaven, for we were with him on the holy mountain" (2 Pet. 1:16–18).

What are glimpses of glory in the Synoptic Gospels become the constant mark of Jesus' ministry in the Fourth Gospel. By his first sign at Cana, Jesus "manifested his glory" (Jn. 2:11). Always Jesus' glory points us to the glory of God. "Yet I do not seek my own glory; there is One who seeks it and he will be the judge" (8:50). Lazarus' illness "is for the glory of God, so that the Son of God may be glorified by means of it" (11:4). At the grave of Lazarus, Jesus says, "Did I not tell you that if you would believe you would see the glory of God?" (11:40). The prayer of ch. 17 is a prayer glorifying the Father and saying, "And now, Father, glorify thou me in thy own presence with the glory which I had with thee before the world was" (17:5).

If God's glory was revealed in the coming and in the ministry of Jesus, it is revealed more clearly in his resurrection. The risen Lord asks disciples on the road to Emmaus, "Was it not necessary that the Christ should suffer these things and enter into his glory?" (Lk. 24:26). Paul says that "Christ was raised from the dead by the glory of the Father" (Rom. 6:4). The rulers of this age did not know what they were doing, "for if they had, they would not have crucified the Lord of glory" (1 Cor. 2:8).

The glory of God is expressed in the risen and exalted Lord of glory. In the hymn of Phil. 2:6–11, God has highly exalted Jesus "and bestowed on him the name which is above every name" and this "to the glory of God the Father." The Ephesian letter exults in what "the God of our Lord Jesus Christ, the Father of glory, . . . accomplished in Christ when he raised him from the dead and made him sit at his right hand in the heavenly places" (Eph. 1:17, 20).

The Epistle to the Hebrews, while recognizing that "we do not yet see everything in subjection to him," goes on to say that "we see Jesus . . . crowned with glory and honor" (Heb. 2:9). Nowhere is the glory of God linked more closely with the glory of the living Christ than in the doxologies of the Apocalypse which combine praise to God with praise to the Lamb. "Worthy art thou, our Lord and God, to receive glory and honor and power" (Rev. 4:11); in the following chapter this becomes the new song of praise to the Lamb. Myriads cry, "Worthy is the Lamb who was slain, to receive power and wealth and wisdom and might and honor and glory and blessing" (5:12).

Easter faith knows that God's glory is seen in the face of Jesus Christ. But this glory is still veiled from those who do not believe, whom the god of this world has kept "from seeing the light of the gospel of the glory of Christ, who is the likeness of God" (2 Cor. 4:4). One day all will see this glory. Easter glory points forward to final glory. He who is "the hope of glory" (Col. 1:27) will be fully revealed as the Lord of glory. The Easter appearances of the risen Lord point forward to his ultimate appearing in glory. Christians are those "awaiting our blessed hope, the appearing of the glory of our great God and Savior Jesus Christ" (Tit. 2:13).

For Luke the ascension is an "eschatological pause" to remind disciples that the present is a time between the times. "This Jesus . . . will come in the same way as you saw him go into heaven" (Acts 1:11). They had seen him until "a cloud took him out of their sight." The cloud is not an elevator. As the Old Testament theophanies make clear (e.g., Ex. 16:10; 19:9; 24:15f.; Num. 9:15; 1 Kings 8:10f.), the cloud expresses the majesty and mystery of God's presence. At the transfiguration, Luke reminded us, "a cloud came and overshadowed them; and they were afraid as they entered the cloud" as a Voice came out of the cloud affirming Jesus as the Son of God (Lk. 9:34f.). Then Jesus had entered the cloud of glory without remaining in it. Now he remains within the cloud and abides forever with God.

In the ascension narrative, as in Daniel's vision of the Son of Man (Dan. 7:13), the clouds "go up" to God's presence. In the apocalyptic discourse, however, Jesus says that all "will see the Son of man coming in a cloud with power and great glory" (Lk. 21:27 and parallels). Then the clouds will "go down" to disclose the ultimate revelation of God.[9] The same motif governs Rev. 1:7 ("Behold, he is coming with the clouds, and every eye will see him, every one who pierced him; and all tribes of the earth will wail on account of him. Even so. Amen "). Easter glory points to the final glory.

VINDICATION AND JUDGMENT

The preceding text indicates that Christ's ultimate appearing in glory will attest God's ultimate vindication of Jesus. God "has fixed a day on which he will judge the world in righteousness by a man whom he has appointed, and of this he has given assurance to all men by raising him from the dead" (Acts 17:31). All people do not yet accept Easter's pledge, but one day "every eye will see him, every one who pierced him" (Rev. 1:7).

This ultimate vindication is expressed in the same imagery we met in our examination of Easter's vindication of Jesus. The future is but the unfolding of what Easter means. The far horizons of consummation, as also those of creation itself, are extrapolated from what God has done in the story of salvation. That is why some Old Testament texts can be linked with the future as well as with the recent past of Jesus' own story.

For example, the language of victorious struggle, drawn from the royal psalms: "Sit at my right hand till I make your enemies your footstool" (Ps. 110:1), is seen as already fulfilled in Eph. 1:22, while 1 Cor. 15:24–25 places this in the future: "Then comes the end, when he delivers the kingdom to God the Father. . . . For he must reign until he has put all his enemies under his feet." The Epistle to the Hebrews cites the parallel "putting everything in subjection under his feet" in Ps. 8:6 as a promise (Heb. 2:8ff.).

Ultimate vindication includes ultimate judgment. The risen Jesus "is the one ordained by God to be judge of the living and the dead" (Acts 10:42; cf. 17:31). This note finds frequent expression in the Synoptic Gospels. "When the Son of man comes in his glory, and all the angels with him, then he will sit on his glorious throne. Before him will be gathered all the nations, and he will separate them one from another as a shepherd separates the sheep from the goats" (Mt. 25: 31–32).

This "last" judgment is but the unfolding of the "past" judgment. Paul says that "there is therefore now no condemnation *(katakrima)* for those who are in Christ Jesus" (Rom. 8:1). But he also says that "we shall all stand before the judgment seat *(bēma)* of God" (Rom. 14:10) or "before the judgment seat *(bēma)* of Christ" (2 Cor. 5:10).

The Fourth Gospel stresses "realized eschatology." "He who believes in him is not condemned *(krinetai);* he who does not believe in him is condemned *(kekritai)* already" (Jn. 3:18). "Now is the judgment *(krisis)* of this world" (12:31). Yet the Gospel links this with a future: "The hour is coming when all who are in the tombs will hear his voice and come forth, those who have done good to the resurrection of life, and those who have done evil to the resurrection of judgment" (5:28–29).

INCARNATION AND THE FUTURE OF JESUS

As an image of the church the Pauline phrase "the body of Christ" calls attention to the corporate Christ who is an "inclusive and all embracing presence."[10] In the following chapter this will be of central importance as we examine the present significance of the resurrection.

Here we are concerned with *Jesus.* Some scholars, notably J. A. T. Robinson, hold that the church is the body of the risen Lord, not metaphorically but "actually." Through the resurrection the church has become "the extension of the Incarnation."[11] Robinson takes the tradition of the empty grave very seriously indeed and certainly allows its historical possibility.[12] But his argument seems to say that the "flesh-body" of the cross is no longer the body of the risen Lord. Because he knows that the empty grave as such does not prove the resurrection, he suggests that "we can be as free to say that the bones of Jesus do *not* lie around Palestine as we can be free to say that they do."[13] The church is now the body, the only body, which the risen Lord has or needs.

Such a view rightly emphasizes that the empty grave cannot prove the resurrection. It also reminds us that we must not equate resurrection with resuscitation. Sometimes the creeds of the church, in their insistence on bodily resurrection, have come close to suggesting resuscitation. In the Thirty-nine Articles of the Church of England (1563) we read: "Christ did truly rise again from the dead, and *took again his body, with flesh, bones, and all things* appertaining to the perfection of Man's nature; wherewith he ascended into heaven and there sitteth, until he return to judge all Men at the last day."[14] So also the Westminster Confession of Faith (1646): "On the third day he arose from the dead, *with the same body* in which he suffered."[15] Such expressions are faithful to the biblical confession that the resurrected Lord is Jesus of Nazareth: "See my hands and my feet, that it is I myself; handle me, and see; for a spirit has not flesh and bones as you see that I have" (Lk. 24:39). Yet this stress on the "same" body in the later creeds does not sufficiently emphasize what the Easter witness of the New Testament also emphasizes—that the body of the risen Lord is "different" because it is a glorified body, not bound by the limitations of our temporal existence.

Withal, simply to identify the body of the risen Lord with the church omits an important theological consideration which the empty grave and the "bodily" appearances of the gospel records are concerned to make. The resurrection is the resurrection of Jesus of Nazareth as an identifiable person, however glorified. The risen Christ is more than the historical Jesus—but he is not less particular and identifiable than the Jesus who died on the cross.

Rather than to say with Robinson that the body of Christ (the church) which Paul has in mind "is as concrete and as singular as the body of the Incarnation,"[16] one may rather say that by the resurrection the incarnation itself (not simply its "extension") continues. Paul does not teach an "immaterial" body but a transformed and glorified body—whether for Christ or for those who are his. "Body" *(sōma)* means "physical body" or "spiritual body." In 1 Corinthians 15, Paul's point is that to deny a resurrection of the body in the future works backward to a view that Christ himself was not raised in body as a whole person. And Paul does not simply identify the body of Christ with the community that finds its life in him. Phil. 3:20–21 makes this clear: "We await a Savior, the Lord Jesus Christ, who will change our lowly body to be like his glorious body."

What of the future? Is the incarnate humanity of Jesus

Christ provisional or permanent?[17] We noted that in 1 Cor. 15: 24–28 Paul says that at the end the Son will deliver the kingdom to God the Father after destroying every adversary. Then, "when all things are subjected to him, the Son himself will also be subjected to him who put all things under him, that God may be everything to every one" (KJV, "all in all"). In the history of doctrine this text has raised the question whether the humanity of Christ is temporary or eternal. In the fourth century, Marcellus of Ancyra understood the kingship of Christ to be inseparable from his humanity. Linking the Pauline text with such passages as Jn. 6:63 ("the flesh is of no avail"), Marcellus held that the incarnation was a temporary accommodation to our need. The humanity of the eternal Logos would continue until the Last Judgment, when "they will look on him whom they pierced." Accordingly, the "until" of 1 Cor. 15:25 points to a time when the incarnation is no longer needed, when the Logos ceases to be the God-man, when he will be "what he was before" so that "God may be all in all." What will happen then to the "flesh" of Christ? Marcellus replied that this is a mystery not revealed in Scripture. Elsewhere, however, he seems to equate this flesh with the church. In any case, the incarnation as such is not eternal. The Second Council of Constantinople anathematized Marcellus and strongly affirmed the future of Jesus Christ, "who will come again with glory to judge the living and the dead," adding, "His kingdom shall have no end."

We call attention to this chapter in the history of doctrine because the suggestion that the humanity of Jesus Christ is a provisional "intermezzo" has had more orthodox formulations than that of Marcellus. Withal, every attempt to limit Jesus' humanity, his "flesh," to his past and not also to his present and future fails to do justice to the New Testament message. Easter revealed Jesus of Nazareth as the Lord. There never will be a time when Jesus is not the incarnate Lord. Paul says that "we shall *always* be with the Lord" (1 Thess. 4:17), and this Lord is Jesus the Christ. Of course, Paul points to a time when "God will be all in all." But how?

An unpublished letter of James Denney put it in striking fashion: "I had rather be found in Christ than lost in God." The future of God cannot ever be sundered from the future of Jesus. "Jesus Christ is the same yesterday and today and for ever" (Heb. 13:8). "Yesterday" points us back to the historic coming, death, resurrection, and ascension of Jesus in the past. "Today" points to his living presence and continuing intercession in the present. "For ever" is not exhausted in the close of the age.

All this reminds us again that the New Testament message sees in Easter the surety of the future of Jesus Christ as Lord of all and Lord forever. In his vision John heard the Easter Christ say, "I am the first and the last, and the living one; I died, and behold I am alive for evermore" (Rev. 1:17–18). He is not only the first, "the beginning of God's [new] creation" (3:14); he is the last, "the Alpha and the Omega, the beginning and the end" (22:13). He is forever the Lamb, the incarnate Christ, who shares forever the eternity of God's glory in the new Jerusalem. Easter faith can no more visualize a terminus for the Lamb than it can for the Lord God who also says, " 'I am the Alpha and the Omega,' . . . who is and who was and who is to come, the Almighty" (1:8).

THE FUTURE OF JESUS
AND THE FUTURE OF ISRAEL[18]

The Synoptic Gospels portray Jesus' poignant yearning for Israel. "Behold, your house is forsaken. And I tell you, you will not see me until you say, 'Blessed is he who comes in the name of the Lord!' " (Lk. 13:35; cf. Mt. 23:38–39). In this perspective we may find a further significance in Matthew's apocalyptic portrayal of the passion to which our attention has already been drawn. "The tombs also were opened, and many bodies of the saints who had fallen asleep were raised, and coming out of the tombs after his resurrection they went into the holy city and appeared to many" (Mt.

27:52–53). Who are these "saints"—and what do they symbolize for the Evangelist?

In the Old Testament we find promises of hope for Israel. "Thy dead shall live, their bodies shall rise. O Dwellers in the dust, awake and sing for joy" (Isa. 26:19). That passage is addressed to "my people" (26:20) and is a song "sung in the land of Judah ... in that day" (26:1). Again, Ezekiel's vision includes a valley of dry bones and God's promise: "Behold, I will open your graves, and raise you from your graves, O my people; and I will bring you home into the land of Israel. And you shall know that I am the Lord when I open your graves, and raise you from your graves, O my people. And I will put my Spirit within you, and you shall live, and I will place you in your own land; then you shall know that I, the Lord, have spoken, and I have done it, says the Lord" (Ezek. 37:12–14). These words were spoken to an Israel which had said, "Our bones are dried up, and our hope is lost; we are clean cut off" (37:11).

Such Old Testament texts may illumine the Evangelist's portrayal. At the cross were those who mocked Jesus in his agony—but God is also there. Jesus had said, "The men of Nineveh will arise at the judgment with this generation and condemn it" (Mt. 12:41). How much more will "the saints" of Israel arise at the judgment of the cross! We conclude that Matthew sees in the resurrected saints a fulfillment of Ezekiel's promised future for Israel.

But how shall we understand the Matthean text: "And all the people answered, 'His blood be on us and on our children!' " (Mt. 27:25)? We know how terribly that text has been misused in Christendom's persecution of the Jews. In Jules Isaac's *Jesus and Israel,* a book written during the Nazi occupation of France, this text is called "the road to Auschwitz."[19] To understand the Evangelist's meaning, however, we need to see that the form of this text parallels that of 2 Sam. 1:16; 3:28–29; and Jer. 51:35, all three texts using the same formula of blood-guiltiness. When Matthew speaks of "all the people," he is not forgetting that Gentiles and Jews

together participated in the crucifixion of Jesus. He is saying
with Paul that "the whole world may be held accountable to
God" (Rom. 3:19).

The church for which Matthew wrote was a church in
which both the links and the tensions between the old and the
new communities of faith (Jews and Jewish-Gentile Christians) required clarification. The newness and freedom of the
Messiah's new community and its links to Israel (e.g., Mt.
17:24–27) needed emphasis. It is an oversimplification and a
mistake to conclude, as Douglas Hare does, that in Matthew's view the future of Israel is only judgment and that
God has finally rejected Israel.[20] The texts we have just cited
do not allow us to say that Matthew's "pessimism concerning
the conversion of Israel is unrelieved by the eschatological
hope found in Paul's treatment of the theme."[21]

Paul's own agony over Israel never entertained the notion
that God has rejected his people (cf. Rom. 11:1). Romans
9–11 is essential to Paul's gospel that the righteousness of
God is also his faithfulness to Israel. "For if their rejection
means the reconciliation of the world, what will their accept-
ance mean but life from the dead?" (Rom. 11:15). This conviction finds its ultimate expression in Paul's confidence that
the "hardening" that has come upon part of Israel was so
that the fullness *(plērōma)* of the Gentiles might come in
"and so all Israel will be saved; as it is written, 'The Deliverer
will come from Zion' " (Rom. 11:26). Indeed, "the gifts and
the call of God are irrevocable. . . . For God has consigned
all to disobedience, that he may have mercy upon *all*" (Rom.
11:29, 32). For Paul's gospel, Israel's future is bound up with
the future of Christ, a mystery that can only be confessed in
doxology and wonder: "O the depth of the riches and wisdom
and knowledge of God! How unsearchable are his judgments
and how inscrutable his ways!" (Rom. 11:33).

Those two wayfaring disciples to whom the risen Lord
appeared on the Emmaus road were not mistaken when they
said, "We had hoped that he was the one to redeem Israel"
(Lk. 24:21). That is why the earliest preaching of the resurrec-

tion in Acts was addressed to Israel. The antithesis, "You killed him . . . but God raised him," is not a rejection of Israel. It is, rather, the antithesis of grace—an invitation and an appeal. Only if the antithesis of grace is true for Israel can it be true for the Gentile world. Peter and Paul, the one who denied and the other who persecuted, are both representatives of Israel. Romans 9–11 is not an isolated passage in the New Testament. The crucified and risen Christ, says the epistle to the Ephesians, "has broken down the dividing wall of hostility." Those who once were alienated from the commonwealth of Israel and had been strangers to the covenants of promise have now been brought near (Eph. 2:11–22). Too often we have spoken of the church as "the new Israel" or "the true Israel." The New Testament does not use such phrases.

While we cannot here develop an appropriate dialogue between the church and Israel,[22] we can let the Easter faith remind us that the future of Jesus includes the future of Israel. When the Evanston Assembly of the World Council of Churches (1954) developed its theme, "Christ the Hope of the World," a legitimate critique of that assembly complained that its study paper ignored the future of Israel—and this for political rather than for theological reasons.[23]

THE FUTURE OF JESUS
AND THE FUTURE OF THE WORLD

The resurrection appearances of Jesus point forward to his ultimate appearing—and this not only in terms of ultimate vindication and judgment but in terms of the redemption of the world. Without forgetting those passages which portray an irrevocable judgment of "the lost," the shape of the New Testament message does not center there. After all, hope can only be expressed positively. Christian hope envisions a day when "every knee shall bow . . . and every tongue confess that Jesus Christ is Lord, to the glory of God the Father." Paul's chapter on the resurrection (1 Corinthians 15) does not speculate on the fate of the lost but speaks rather of Christ as the second Adam. "For as in Adam *all* die, so also in Christ shall *all* be made alive" (15:22). Such a vision is also the summation of Romans 9 to 11. "God has consigned *all* to disobedience, that he may have mercy upon *all*" (Rom. 11:32). How God's loving purpose and his righteous judgment are united we cannot know. Hope in God does not encourage speculation—whether in terms of universalism or in terms of particularism. Hope in God is trust in God. "By his great mercy we have been born anew to a living hope through the resurrection of Jesus Christ from the dead" (1 Pet. 1:3). A recent creedal statement says what can be said:

> We live in tension between God's warnings and promises.
> Knowing the righteous judgment of God in Christ,
>   we urge all people to be reconciled to God,
>   not exempting ourselves from the warnings.
> Constrained by God's love in Christ,
>   we have good hope for all people,
>   not exempting the most unlikely from the promises.
> Judgment belongs to God and not to us.
> We are sure that God's future for every person
>   will be both merciful and just."[24]

In the apocalyptic discourse Jesus said: "And this gospel of the kingdom will be preached throughout the whole world, as a testimony to all nations; and then the end will come" (Mt. 24:14). That same Evangelist closes his Easter chapter with the words of the risen Lord: "All authority in heaven and on earth has been given to me. Go therefore and make disciples of all nations" (28:18–19). In both verses, the word rendered "nations" is *ethnē*, which may be rendered as "the Gentiles." Not only Israel but "all the Gentiles" *(panta ta ethnē)* are to receive the good news of the gospel.

Thus the Lord of the future calls his followers to participate in his future which is the fulfilling of his mission in all the world. "Go therefore." The best description of evangelism is "hope in action."[25]

The future of humankind points to the future of the creation. "We wait for new heavens and a new earth in which righteousness dwells" (2 Pet. 3:13). Creation and consummation find their key in the future of Jesus Christ. "For in him all the fulness of God was pleased to dwell, and through him to reconcile to himself *all things,* whether on earth or in heaven, making peace by the blood of his cross" (Col. 1: 19–20). God "has made known to us in all wisdom and insight the mystery of his will, according to his purpose which he set forth in Christ as a plan for the fulness of time, to unite *all things* in him, things in heaven and things on earth" (Eph. 1:9–10).

Such is the breathtaking scope of what the New Testament message sees in the resurrection of Jesus Christ. The vision of the future extends from *pantes* ("all persons") to *ta panta* ("all things"). Only in this larger perspective is it appropriate to speak of our own future in Christ. To this we now turn.

THE RESURRECTION OF JESUS AND OUR RESURRECTION

We have maintained that the Easter faith represents something so new and unprecedented that apocalyptic tradition of a final resurrection of the dead could not have created it. Apocalyptic tradition provided the language to describe the Christian confession that God had raised one man, Jesus of Nazareth, in the middle of the times—but Easter faith itself represents something quite unprecedented.

Now, as we consider "the resurrection of the dead" (plural) at the end of the age, we must ask whether this hope also is dependent on the unprecedented resurrection of Jesus or whether Jewish tradition is sufficient to account for it.

As noted earlier, Paul's argument in 1 Corinthians 15 appears circular. "If the dead are not raised, then Christ has not been raised" (15:16). On the other hand, "If Christ has not been raised, . . . then those also who have fallen asleep in Christ have perished" (15:17–18).

Sometimes it would seem that the hope of final resurrection can stand on its own. We are to "rely not on ourselves but on God who raises the dead" (2 Cor. 1:9). The promise to Abraham was given "in the presence of the God in whom he believed, who gives life to the dead" (Rom. 4:17). Kegel[26] has suggested that in such texts Paul is citing a general Jewish confession such as the Second Benediction of the *Schmone Esre* rather than expressing distinctively Christian data. At least from the period after A.D. 70, and probably earlier, this anti-Sadducean prayer sought to engrave on Jewish minds the doctrine of the resurrection. It includes:

> Thou art mighty for ever, Jahweh, thou quickenest the dead, thou art mighty to save . . . and keepest faith to those that sleep in the dust . . . who killest and quickenest, and causest salvation to spring forth. And faithful art thou to quicken the dead. Blessed be thou, Jahweh, who quickenest the dead.[27]

For that matter, Jesus' reply to the Sadducean denial of the resurrection is understandable in the religious setting of his own time without reference to Easter. And Luke singles out the Sadducees rather than the Pharisees as the opponents of Paul's Easter faith, suggesting that Paul is on trial for the faith of his fathers. In view of such considerations, can one maintain that the New Testament witness to the resurrection of the dead at the final day is dependent on the resurrection of Jesus?

A good deal depends on whether we can assume that the Pharisaic belief in a future resurrection was a common rather than a particular expression of Jewish belief in the first century. Because the Sadducees were the losing party after A.D. 70, it does not necessarily follow that their denial of a future resurrection was a minority opinion in the days of Jesus. We do not know. Studies in the Dead Sea Scrolls have not established clear evidence that belief in the resurrection was prominent in that apocalyptically oriented community. In the Wisdom of Solomon we find expressions of immortality rather than of resurrection. Late Judaism included a wide variety of views about death and what follows. After collecting all the available evidence from the Jewish background, H. C. C. Cavallin concludes that to speak of "the" Jewish doctrine of the resurrection of the dead, and more particularly of resurrection of the body, is indeed a "myth."[28]

Nonetheless, without forgetting the wide diversity of Jewish views about the future, it is clear that faith in a God who raises the dead at the last day is not a Christian novelty but has its roots in Israel's faith. For both Jew and Christian, this hope was not so much an individualistic hope of survival as a communal hope, a trust that God would save his people.

But the newness of the New Testament need not be novelty. In Christ all things have become new—including the hope of the future. For one thing, the communal scope of the hope is enlarged. The resurrection of Jesus is seen as the fulfillment of the promise to Abraham, a promise that is enlarged because Abraham is "the father of many nations" *(pollōn ethnōn)* and thus of Gentiles who never lived under the Mosaic covenant (Rom. 4:16ff.).

The scope of God's coming salvation is not only enlarged, it now receives its surety and shape in the resurrection of Jesus. "For since we believe that Jesus died and rose again, even so, through Jesus, God will bring with him those who have fallen asleep" (1 Thess. 4:14). For now "Christ has been raised from the dead, the first fruits of those who have fallen asleep" (1 Cor. 15:20). The order is "Christ the first fruits, then at his coming those who belong to Christ" (1 Cor. 15:23).

This image of "first fruits" can be applied both to the risen Christ and to his community. James says that of his own will God has "brought us forth by the word of truth that we should be a kind of first fruits of his creatures" (James 1:18). The seer of Patmos "looked, and lo, on Mount Zion stood the Lamb, and with him a hundred and forty-four thousand who had his name and his Father's name written on their foreheads" and who sing the new song because they "have been redeemed from mankind as first fruits for God and the Lamb" (Rev. 14:1–4). Again, Christ's followers, whether

Paul's beloved Epaenetus who is the firstfruits of Asia for Christ (Rom. 16:5) or the martyrs of the Apocalypse, are the "first fruits" of a redeemed humanity.

The new shape of hope can be expressed in a variety of ways. It is an inheritance, as in the doxology of 1 Pet. 1:3–5. "Blessed be the God and Father of our Lord Jesus Christ! By his great mercy we have been born anew to a living hope through the resurrection of Jesus Christ from the dead, and to an inheritance which is imperishable, undefiled, and unfading, kept in heaven for you, who by God's power are guarded through faith for a salvation ready to be revealed in the last time."

It finds expression also in the imagery of seeing Christ. "Beloved, we are God's children now; it does not yet appear what we shall be, but we know that when he appears we shall be like him, for we shall see him as he is" (1 Jn. 3:2). The writer's "we shall see him" is linked with his initial reminder of "that which was from the beginning, which we have heard, which we have seen with our eyes, which we have looked upon and touched with our hands, concerning the word of life" (1:1). Fellowship with the Father and with his Son Jesus Christ is the pledge of fuller fellowship in the future.

And so we come to the resurrection of the dead. We have noted the many texts that see in the resurrection of Jesus the dawning of the end time. We have seen how this needed to be guarded as hope, lest people fall into the illusion that they can dispense with the "not yet" of the future. Easter is the pledge of the future life with Christ. "For if we have been united with him in a death like his, we shall certainly be united with him in a resurrection like his" (Rom. 6:5).

This is the burden of 1 Corinthians 15. "Now if Christ is preached as raised from the dead, how can some of you say that there is no resurrection of the dead?" (15:12). But how to conceive this future? Without attempting here a sufficient exposition of Paul's chapter on the resurrection, we can note that Paul guards against any notion that resurrection is resuscitation or that eternal life is simply the prolongation of this life. He is equally concerned to guard against any suggestion that life to come, any more than life now, can dispense with body. The risen Lord is some*body,* not no*body.* He is forever the crucified and risen one. It is not different with us. To the question, "How are the dead raised? With what kind of body do they come?" (15:35), Paul only affirms that "God gives it a body as he has chosen" (15:38). The body of the future is a "spiritual body."

In 2 Cor. 5:3, Paul says that we shall not be found "naked." It may be that Paul's thought develops. Moule suggests that in 1 Corinthians 15, Paul believed that matter would be included in or enclosed and swallowed up by a superimposed immortality, while in 2 Corinthians 4 to 5 he suggests that matter must be surrendered and released in exchange for what transcends it.[29] In any case:

> Paul steered a remarkably consistent course between, on the one hand, a materialistic doctrine of physical resurrection and, on the other hand, a dualistic doctrine of escape of the soul from the body, and the secret of this consistency is his tenacious grasp of the central theme: Jesus, Son of God.[30]

Paul speaks of selfhood transformed, not of selfhood lost. "But our commonwealth is in heaven, and from it we await a Savior, the Lord Jesus Christ, who will change [transform] our lowly body to be like his glorious body, by the power which enables him even to subject all things to himself" (Phil. 3:20–21).

If we ask how Paul's conception of a "spiritual body" and his statement that "flesh and blood cannot inherit the kingdom of God" (1 Cor. 15:50) are compatible with the Lukan and Johannine portrayals of the risen Jesus' "same" body, we need not simply point to the diversity of the New Testament witness to the resurrection, diverse as this may be. The Easter narratives that most emphasize "bodily" resurrection also stress the transformed nature of this body. The risen Lord is not a Lazarus returned to earthly life. Neither is Lazarus a paradigm for what we will be.

Withal, the New Testament message is not concerned to speculate about the nature of the resurrection body.[31] The New Testament writers do not deal with the resurrection of the body in a purely individualistic manner, for the Christian hope of resurrection is a social hope. That is one reason why Paul disavows speculative questions about the resurrection body in 1 Corinthians 15.[32]

It is enough for Christians to "wait for adoption as sons, the redemption of our bodies. For in this hope we were saved. Now hope that is seen is not hope. For who hopes for what he sees? But if we hope for what we do not see, we wait for it with patience" (Rom. 8:23–25).

Without Easter, history is a journey through the shadows, as it was for those travelers to Emmaus. "But we *had hoped* that he was the one to redeem Israel" (Lk. 24:21). Dante has some haunting words for those who enter hell: "Abandon hope, all ye who enter here!" Indeed, "hell is hopelessness."[33] But Easter sent those travelers back to Jerusalem in a return that one can describe in the words of an Old Testament promise: "Return to your stronghold, O prisoners of hope; today I declare that I will restore to you double" (Zech. 9:12). Prisoners of hope! The future is the unfolding of what happened at Easter.

In his *Theology of Hope,* Jürgen Moltmann wrote:

> But how, then, can Christian eschatology give expression to the future? Christian eschatology does not speak of the future as such. It sets out from a definite reality in history and announces the future of that reality, its future possibilities and its power over the future. Christian eschatology speaks of Jesus Christ and *his* future. It recognizes the reality of the raising of Jesus and proclaims the future of the risen Lord. Hence the question whether all statements about the future are grounded in the person and history of Jesus Christ provides it with the touchstone by which to distinguish the spirit of eschatology from that of utopia.[34]

He continued:

> Without faith's knowledge of Christ, hope becomes a utopia and remains hanging in the air. But without hope, faith falls to pieces, becomes a fainthearted and ultimately a dead faith. It is through faith that man finds the path of true life, but it is only hope that keeps him on that path.[35]

That path of life leads us to the significance of the Easter faith for the present—for the living of these days.

IV

The Significance
of the Resurrection
for the Present

We live between the past and the future. Accordingly, we turn to the New Testament message of the resurrection to see how Easter shapes the worship and work of the church today.

Verb tenses can be illuminating. In Isaiah 40–55, the prophet of the exile recites God's past acts of creation and redemption through verb tenses that turn this recital into a proclamation of God's present and coming acts of deliverance.[1] The RSV (as also the NEB) renders the perfect tenses in one passage (Isa. 49:8):

> In a time of favor I have answered you,
>   in a day of salvation I have helped you.

The Jerusalem Bible puts these in the future:

> At the favourable time I will answer you,
>   on the day of salvation I will help you.

The New American Bible (and a number of recent commentators)[2] uses the present:

> In a time of favor I answer you,
>   on the day of salvation I help you.

In describing the ministry of reconciliation, Paul cites the prophetic word as he found it in the Greek Old Testament (which uses the aorist past tense):

> At the acceptable time I have listened to you,
> and helped you on the day of salvation.

Paul adds, "Behold, *now* is the acceptable time; behold, *now* is the day of salvation" (2 Cor. 6:2).

The "third day" and the "last day" stamp "this day" as "the day of salvation."

It is instructive to note the verb tenses in various Pauline passages. For example, in the baptismal imagery of Rom. 6:3–11, Paul points to the Christian life as lived between a "no longer" and a "not yet." The past and future tenses are prominent:

> Do you not know that all of us who *have been baptized* into Christ Jesus *were baptized* into his death? We *were buried* therefore *with* him by baptism into death, so that as Christ *was raised* from the dead by the glory of the Father, we too might walk in newness of life. For if we *have been united with* him in a death like his, we *shall* certainly *be united with* him in a resurrection like his. . . . But if we *have died* with Christ, we believe that we *shall* also *live with* him."

This baptismal imagery returns in Col. 2:12, but with a change in verb tense:

> You *were buried with* him in baptism [here the tense is the same as in Romans 6], in which you *were* also *raised with* him through faith in the working of God, who *raised* him from the dead.

In Col. 3:1, the ethical appeal begins: "If then you *have been raised with* Christ, seek the things that are above, where Christ is." In Eph. 2:5, this note finds even stronger expression: God *"has made* us *alive together with* Christ . . . and *raised* us *up with* him . . . and *made* us *sit with* him in the heavenly places in Christ Jesus."

This shift in tenses (future/past) should not surprise us.[3] The reality of the new life must have had a beginning, and it "is only natural that we should find texts which speak of our resurrection with Christ to new life as a past event."[4] But the reality of this new life is not confused with its consummation, hence the future tense. "When Christ who is our life appears, then you also *will appear* with him in glory" (Col. 3:4). We live between a "no longer" and a "not yet."

The Pauline "no longer" finds its most forceful expression in the statement that "if anyone is in Christ, that person is a new creation; the old has passed away, behold, the new has come" (2 Cor. 5:17). For "the love of Christ controls us, because we are convinced that one has died for all; therefore all have died. And he died for all, that those who live might live no longer for themselves but for him who for their sake died and was raised" (5:14–15). But the "no longer" does not forget the "not yet." Paul's hope is "that I may know him and the power of his resurrection, and may share his sufferings, becoming like him in his death, that if possible I may attain the resurrection from the dead" (Phil. 3:10–11).

The Lord who appeared at Easter and who will appear at the end is the Lord who is present today.

How is he present? The Easter appearances have ended. "Without having seen him you love him; though you do not now see him you believe in him and rejoice with unutterable and exalted joy" (1 Pet. 1:8). In John's Easter chapter, the risen Lord says to Thomas: "Have you believed because you have seen me? Blessed are those who have not seen and yet believe" (Jn. 20:29). The Evangelist is not criticizing the "seeing" of the first witnesses.[5] He is addressing those who, like ourselves, were not present in that unrepeatable first Easter. Throughout the Fourth Gospel, as Raymond Brown puts it, the Evangelist

> has had in mind an audience seated in the darkened theater of the future, silently viewing what Jesus was saying and doing. True to the limitations and logic of the stage drama imposed by the Gospel form, the Johannine Jesus could address that audience only indirectly through the disciples who shared the stage and gave voice to the sentiments and reactions that were shared by the audience as well. But now, as the curtain is about to fall on the stage drama, the lights in the theater are suddenly turned on. Jesus shifts his attention from the disciples on the stage to

the audience that has become visible and makes clear that his
ultimate concern is for them—those who have come to believe
in him through the word of his disciples (xvii 20).[6]

How is Easter a present reality? How is the risen Lord
present today?

THE RISEN CHRIST AND THE SPIRIT

THE SPIRIT: GOD'S PRESENCE AND POWER

We begin with some general comments. When the Bible
speaks of the Spirit of God or the Holy Spirit, it speaks of
God as Spirit, God as presence and power.

The Hebrew word *ruach,* as the Greek word *pneuma,*
suggests an imagery of air in motion. When the imagery is
drawn from the realm of nature, it suggests "wind." In Gen.
1:2, the RSV renders *ruach* as "spirit" ("and the Spirit of
God was moving over the face of the waters"); the NEB
renders it as "wind" ("and a mighty wind swept over the
surface of the waters"). In Jn. 3:8, Jesus used the analogy of
wind and spirit in his conversation with Nicodemus: "the
wind *(to pneuma)* blows where it wills; . . . so it is with every
one who is born of the Spirit *(ek tou pneumatos).*" It is
entirely appropriate that in Luke's portrayal of Pentecost the
gift of the Spirit should be attended by a sound from heaven
like the rushing of a mighty wind *(pnoē).*

On the other hand, when the imagery is drawn from the
realm of intelligent nature, the meaning is "breath" and this
is not far removed from "word." An example is Ps. 33:6.

> By the word of the Lord the heavens were made,
>   and all their host by the breath *(ruach)* of his mouth.

The creative Spirit is also the re-creative Spirit who imparts
new life by blowing on the valley of dry bones (Ezekiel 37).
"Come from the four winds, O breath *(ruach),* and breathe
upon these slain, that they may live" (37:9. The RSV footnote
reminds us that "breath" can also be rendered here as "wind"

or "spirit"). In Berkhof's words, "Ezekiel sees that in the last days God will perform a new creative act, similar to what he did to Adam."[7] Joel envisions a time when God "will pour out" his Spirit on all flesh (Joel 2:28). God promises the mysterious Servant of the Lord: "I have put my Spirit upon him" (Isa. 42:1). Of the promised Messiah we read, "And the Spirit of the Lord shall rest upon him" (Isa. 11:2).

The Spirit of God is God in creative and re-creative power and presence. The New Testament declares that God was present in Jesus of Nazareth as in no one else. Jesus was anointed by the Spirit. He was led by the Spirit. He was full of the Spirit. At Nazareth he began his ministry by saying, "The Spirit of the Lord is upon me, because he has anointed me" (Lk. 4:18). The Spirit was evident in his work as well as in his word. "If it is by the Spirit of God that I cast out demons, then the kingdom of God has come upon you" (Mt. 12:28; the parallel in Lk. 11:20, "If it is by the finger of God . . .", uses another Old Testament expression for the power and presence of God: cf. Ex. 8:19). Jesus was uniquely the bearer of the Spirit in his word and in his work because "God was with him" (Acts 10:38) in unprecedented manner.

Easter faith affirms that this Jesus, vindicated by the Spirit through the resurrection (Rom. 1:4; 1 Tim. 3:16), is now not only the bearer but the giver and sender of the Spirit. In John's Easter chapter, "he breathed on them, and said to them, 'Receive the Holy Spirit' " (Jn. 20:22). In Luke, as we have seen, the risen Lord promised the Spirit at Easter and, as the ascended Lord, bestowed the Spirit at Pentecost. In both traditions he is the sender of the Spirit.

Berkhof reminds us that these two aspects, bearer and sender, are not contradictory but are complementary. "We even find them together in one sentence in Jn. 1:33, where God says to John the Baptist: 'He on whom you see the Spirit descend and remain, this is he who baptizes with the Holy Spirit.' . . . Jesus can be the sender of the Spirit only because he is first the receiver and bearer of the Spirit. . . . The Spirit rests on Jesus and the Spirit goes out from Jesus."[8]

LORD AND SPIRIT

The Spirit is the action of the exalted Christ. In Acts 16:7, the Spirit is "the Spirit of Jesus." In 1 Pet. 1:11, the Spirit is "the Spirit of Christ" and, somewhat like Luke, the writer speaks of "the Holy Spirit sent from heaven." In the Fourth Gospel, Jesus, when pointing to the sending of the Spirit, says: "I will not leave you desolate; I will come to you" (Jn. 14:18). In 1 Jn. 3:24 we read: "And by this we know that he [Christ] abides in us, by the Spirit which he has given us."

Does this mean that the New Testament identifies the exalted Lord with the Spirit? Some passages might suggest this. In Rom. 8:9–11, the One who indwells the Christian community is variously called the Spirit, the Spirit of God, the Spirit of Christ, and Christ himself.

> But you are not in the flesh, you are in the Spirit, if in fact the Spirit of God dwells in you. Any one who does not have the Spirit of Christ does not belong to him. But if Christ is in you, although your bodies are dead because of sin, your spirits are alive because of righteousness. If the Spirit of him who raised Jesus from the dead dwells in you, he who raised Christ Jesus from the dead will give life to your mortal bodies also through his Spirit which dwells in you.

Does Paul identify Lord and Spirit? We turn to other Pauline passages that can help our interpretation.

One passage often cited is 1 Cor. 15:45: "Thus it is written, 'The first man Adam became a living being *(egeneto . . . eis psychēn zōsan),* the last Adam became a life-giving Spirit *(egeneto . . . eis pneuma zōopoioun).*' " On this verse James Dunn comments: "Not only is the earthly Jesus lost in the shadows of the exalted Lord, but the exalted Lord seems to be wholly identified with the Spirit, the source of the new life experienced by believers."[9] We should note, however, that in this passage the stress is not on the relationship of Lord and Spirit but on the contrast between the physical body and the spiritual body. The exalted Christ not only has a spiritual body but is himself the life-giver, in contrast to the first man who became a living being (Paul is quoting the Greek version of Gen. 2:7 *(kai egeneto ho anthrōpos eis psychēn zōsan)*. Paul views the first and the last Adam as inclusive figures (as in Romans 5) in whom we see the whole of human history.

A better text for identifying Lord and Spirit seems to be 2 Cor. 3:17–18: "Now the Lord is the Spirit. . . . This comes from the Lord who is the Spirit" *(ho de kyrios to pneuma estin . . . kathaper apo kyriou pneumatos)*. At first sight this would seem conclusive. Most scholars[10] assume that "Lord" here must be the "Lord Jesus," because this is Paul's usual terminology. Is this so?

Dunn and Moule[11] have argued persuasively that in the context of this passage "the Lord" must be understood as the Lord Yahweh. The whole passage is a kind of "homily" on Exodus 34. If so, the climax of the passage comes when Paul says that the Lord of the exodus story is for us no longer remote on a mountain but is, through Christ, the Spirit in our midst. This is how the Old Testament promise is fulfilled that God would dwell with his people. The glory of the Lord no longer wanes—as in the exodus story—but rather increases as people are being transformed into God's likeness from one degree of glory to another.

Withal, the Spirit is not simply another name for the exalted Christ. The Spirit is the Spirit *of* Christ. The preposition not only points to an inseparable relationship between the Spirit and Christ, it also points to a distinction. We must not minimize the inseparable bond between Lord and Spirit. To be "in Christ" is to be "in the Spirit." But the Lord of glory transcends his own work as the life-giving Spirit. In Berkhof's words: "He is eternally in the glory of the Father as the first fruits of mankind, as the guarantee of our future, as the advocate of the church. His life, as the life of the One in whom the goal of humanity is attained, is more than his function toward us."[12] The consummation will be more than the present. That is why "the Spirit and the Bride [the church] say, 'Come' " (Rev. 22:17).

The risen Lord indwells and empowers his followers

through his Spirit. The bond between Lord and Spirit makes it possible for New Testament faith to say that Christ is both at the right hand of the Father and also present in our midst. His transcendence is not lost in his immanence.

Our concern here is not speculative but experiential. We are examining the New Testament texts to see how the Spirit is the earthly presence and action of the risen Lord.

THE SPIRIT AS THE ACTION
OF THE RISEN LORD

Shall we begin with the mission of the risen Christ in the world through his Spirit, or with his equipping and empowering his community for the mission?[13] Shall we begin with the community or with the individual Christian? The latter question is more easily answered than the former. To be "in Christ" or "in the Spirit" is, especially in Pauline theology, a communal reality. The "you" in Rom. 8:9–11 is plural. "It is this communal dimension," says Peter Selby, "which is lacking in so many contemporary versions of the resurrection faith."[14] That is why our discussion will move from "The Risen Christ and the Spirit" to "The Risen Christ and the Church."

For the moment, it is enough to remind ourselves that Christ's work in heaven and his work on earth constitute one work. We have seen that *intercession* is part of that work. Paul says that Christ, the only one who has the right to condemn us, is actually at the right hand of God and "indeed intercedes for us" (Rom. 8:34). He "pleads our cause" (NEB). We have seen how The Epistle to the Hebrews portrays this intercession as Christ's high-priestly work—that the exalted Lord is "able for all time to save those who draw near to God through him, since he always lives to make intercession for them" (Heb. 7:25).

Yet we must not think of this intercession as a remote activity. Paul says that the Spirit helps us in our weak praying because the Spirit "intercedes for us" (Rom. 8:26). The NEB has the best rendering: "Through our inarticulate groans the

Spirit himself is pleading for us, and God who searches our inmost being knows what the Spirit means, because he pleads for God's people in God's own way." The initiative in prayer is God's. "Lord and Spirit" means that God is for us and with us.

Johannine theology, as we have seen, expresses this same work in terms of *advocacy*. If we sin—and who does not?— "we have an advocate *(paraklētos)* with the Father, Jesus Christ the righteous" (1 Jn. 2:1). The Son who is with the Father in glory has not left us orphans (Jn. 14:18). Jesus says that he will pray the Father to "give you *another* counselor *(paraklētos)* to be with you for ever" (14:16). This advocate and counselor is "the Spirit of truth" (14:17), "the Holy Spirit," who "will teach you all things, and bring to your remembrance all that I have said to you" (14:26). It is by Jesus' "going away" that the *paraklētos* comes to convince the world concerning sin and righteousness and judgment (16:8ff.). While on earth Jesus had convinced the world of sin and of righteousness and of judgment. That ministry continues through the Spirit. Jesus' promise is fulfilled when at Easter the risen Lord says: "Receive the Holy Spirit. If you forgive the sins of any, they are forgiven; if you retain the sins of any, they are retained" (20:22–23).[15]

Christ's work in heaven and his work on earth constitute one work. Every one of the seven letters to the churches in the Apocalypse is a letter of the risen Lord (e.g., "The words of the first and the last, who died and came to life," Rev. 2:8). Every one of these letters closes with the words, "He who has an ear, let him hear what the Spirit says to the churches." Without positing any literary relationship between the Apocalypse and the Fourth Gospel, one can say that this link between risen Lord and Spirit is congruous with what the Johannine Jesus says: "When the Spirit of truth comes, he will guide you into all the truth; for he will not speak on his own authority, but whatever he hears he will speak, and he will declare to you the things that are to come. He will glorify me, for he will take what is mine and declare it to you" (Jn. 16:13–14).

THE SPIRIT BEARS WITNESS
TO THE LORD

This Johannine reminder deserves particular emphasis. "But when the Counselor *(parakletos)* comes, whom I shall send to you from the Father, even the Spirit of truth, who proceeds from the Father, he will bear witness to me" (Jn. 15:26). The Spirit is never separated from the Lord, for the Spirit is the Spirit of Christ. Commenting on these Paraclete sayings of the Fourth Gospel, Hendry writes:

> The work of the Spirit is essentially of a reproductive nature; it has always to do with the work of the incarnate Christ. The Paraclete sayings lay marked stress on the unoriginality of the Spirit's work: this work, if we may so express it, is simply to hold the spotlight on Christ, to glorify him by taking what is his and showing it to his disciples (John 16:14). The Spirit is to be remembrancer (ch. 14:26), not innovator.... In a word, it is the function of the Spirit, according to the Johannine teaching, to re-present the truth that is in Christ.[16]

At Pentecost, when people asked, "What does this mean?" (Acts 2:12), Peter did not reply with a discourse on the Spirit but with a sermon proclaiming Jesus as the risen Lord.

The Spirit bears witness that "Jesus is Lord." In this connection, it is useful to consider 1 Cor. 12:3, where Paul says that "no one speaking by the Spirit of God ever says 'Jesus be cursed!' *(Anathema Iesous)* and no one can say 'Jesus is Lord' *(Kyrios Iesous)* except by the Holy Spirit."

Why this warning? Interpreters often suggest that Paul was warning against some Gnostic or other "spiritual" disavowal of the humanity of Jesus. W. C. van Unnik has offered a quite different interpretation. If Paul himself was ready to be *anathema* for the sake of his fellow Israelites (Rom. 9:3), and if, in Gal. 3:13, he could say that Christ himself had become a "curse" *(katara),* why is it inappropriate to call

Jesus *anathema?* In biblical speech, *anathema* is a means to remove sin; *kyrios* is the one who grants salvation. Why are the two put in opposition here? *Anathema* implies the total destruction of him on whom it rests. *Kyrios* is the name of him whom God has raised from the dead.

> *Anathema,* says Paul, cannot be said of Jesus, because although he died on the cross, and for that reason could be called a curse, would imply his annihilation and separation from God. It would be an implicit denial of his resurrection (cf. I Cor. 15 and particularly verse 12). But the Christian believed in and confessed Jesus as *Kyrios.* [17]

We have become so accustomed to saying "Jesus is Lord," he adds, that we are hardly aware of what a tremendous step is involved. That Jesus of Nazareth had been crucified was a hard, historic fact that could have been seen by anyone. But that Jesus Christ is the risen and exalted Lord could not possibly be verified by the "natural man" (1 Cor. 2:14). This "lies outside the boundaries of human observation. . . . It is only by a special revelation that one can know what has been done to Jesus by God, namely that he has become Lord. But then it also follows that to acknowledge Jesus as *Kyrios* is a work of the Holy Spirit." [18] That is why "no one speaking by the Spirit of God ever says 'Jesus *Anathema'* and no one can say 'Jesus is Lord' except by the Holy Spirit." The Spirit bears witness to the risen Lord.

A NOTE ON THE TRINITY

In the New Testament, God reveals himself to us as Father in the Son and through the Spirit. Formulas such as the threefold baptismal name (Mt. 28:19) and the threefold apostolic benediction (2 Cor. 13:14) express what is implicit in the Gospels (e.g., Jn. 14:26; 14:16f.), in Acts (e.g., Acts 2:33), and in the epistles (e.g., 1 Cor. 12:4ff.).

The creedal formulation of the Trinity belongs to the history of doctrine rather than to a theology of the New Testament. Through the controversies over the meaning of

Christ's divinity, the church came to see that what was said of the Son had to be said of the Spirit's divinity if the church's confession of faith is to be true to the biblical revelation. We cannot review that history here.[19] Words such as *persona* ("person") and *hypostasis* ("subsistence") had meanings then that often led to confusion. They were and are less than adequate to express the unity of the God who has revealed himself as Father, Son, and Spirit.

We can say that "Father," "Son," and "Spirit" are relational terms to describe the one God's self-revelation and outreach to his creation. "We have nothing to do with a nature of God outside his revelation. We may believe that he is as his revelation is."[20] His outreach is not only a history for us, "it is also a history within God himself. His movement is not outside of himself."[21]

In his recent Bampton Lectures, *God as Spirit,* G. W. H. Lampe proposes an interpretation of the resurrection very different from that of our foregoing pages. His view entails a radical reconstruction of trinitarian doctrine. He rejects a bodily resurrection of Jesus and "post-existent Christ" (as also a "pre-existent Christ") because for him the resurrection "is the broadening out of the union of God's Spirit with man from its embodiment in the individual life of Jesus to include all those who are indwelt and taught and guided into all the truth by the Spirit that was his. . . . Resurrection is the liberation of the life of the individual Jesus to become the life of all men whom God's Spirit that was in him refashions according to his likeness."[22] Our participation in Christ's Sonship "does not seem in any way to depend on whether a resurrection-event actually happened. . . . We are freed from the impossible task of distinguishing the presence of Christ from the presence of the Spirit, of defining what is meant by a Christian's encounter with a personal Jesus, and of determining the role of the Holy Spirit as a 'third person,' additional to the personal and post-existent Christ."[23]

While this provocative book has raised some searching questions for traditional formulations, something central in

New Testament faith is lost when Jesus himself has no continuing identity as the risen Lord, when he himself becomes a figure of the past whose life revealed what we may be.

THE RISEN CHRIST AND THE CHURCH

Having said that the Spirit is the mode of the risen Lord's presence and action on earth, we must go on to say that this presence is not abstract but finds a visible expression in the community of Christ. "Lord and Spirit" lead us to "Lord and Church."

THE CHURCH AS THE BODY OF CHRIST

Of the many biblical images of the church,[24] the Pauline image of "the body of Christ" has received particular attention[25] and has important bearing on our study of the resurrection.

A detailed examination of the image is beyond the scope of this chapter.[26] In the earlier epistles (Corinthians and Romans), the stress is on the mutual relationships within the body. "For just as the body is one and has many members, and all the members of the body, though many, are one body, so it is with Christ" (1 Cor. 12:12). "The body does not consist of one member but of many" (12:14). "As it is, there are many parts, yet one body" (12:20). "Now you are the body of Christ and individually members of it" (12:27). "For as in one body we have many members, and all the members do not have the same function, so we, though many, are one body in Christ, and individually members one of another" (Rom. 12:4–5).

In the later epistles (Colossians and Ephesians), the image is expanded to stress the relationship of the body to its head. Christ "is the head of the body, the church" (Col. 1:18). Indeed, God "has made him the head over all things for the church, which is his body, the fulness of him who fills all in all" (Eph. 1:22–23).

These are but some of the texts. A more complete description would examine texts that deal with the crucified body given for us and with the eucharistic texts (e.g., 1 Corinthians 10 to 11). Our concern here is limited to the church as the body of Christ. In the previous chapter it was suggested that the New Testament data do not allow us so to identify the church with the resurrection body of Christ that the church becomes the extension of the incarnation. Paul's use of "body" imagery is fluid rather than fixed or uniform.[27] Christ's "body of glory" (Phil. 3:21) is certainly not the church. Again, in 1 Cor. 12:21, "head" does not denote Christ but simply one of the members of the body, whereas in the later epistles Christ is the "head." Moreover, if Paul says that "you *are* the body of Christ," he also says that "you *are* God's field, God's building" (1 Cor. 3:9). These are certainly metaphors, as is the nuptual image: "I betrothed you, a pure virgin, to one husband, to present you to Christ" (2 Cor. 11:2, so Ernest Best; the Greek text does not have the "as" which is added in the translations).

We conclude that the image of the church as Christ's body is to be understood in metaphorical rather than in "realistic" manner. This does not demean its importance. The church "is not identical with him; but is not separate from him."[28]

THE CORPORATE CHRIST

This last reminder needs further attention. For Paul, Christ as the last Adam is an inclusive and corporate personality in whom the one and the many are forever united. Whatever antecedents one may find in backgrounds such as the Old Testament conceptions of corporate personality (in which racial or religious solidarity enables one to see the many in the one), this assumes an unprecedented importance in the New Testament's interpretation of the risen Christ, especially in some of the Pauline texts on "the body of Christ." Augustine often spoke of the *totus Christus* ("the whole Christ") to stress that the whole Christ is made up of the Head and the Members of the body. "The whole Christ is the head and the body: the head, that Saviour of the body, has already ascended into heaven, but the body is the Church which toils on earth."[29]

In other New Testament writers the individual identity of the risen Jesus is emphasized more than the corporate Christ. For example, Luke's ascension narrative places the locus of the risen Christ in heaven rather than on earth. Yet it is worth noting that in Luke's three accounts of Paul's encounter with the heavenly Christ, the Voice from heaven says to him: "Saul, Saul, why do you persecute *me?*. . . . I am Jesus [or, Jesus of Nazareth], whom you are persecuting" (Acts 9:4f.; 22:7f.; 26:15f.). In persecuting Christ's followers, Paul was persecuting Christ himself. Afterward the persecutor becomes himself the persecuted. Paul goes to Jerusalem "bound in the Spirit, not knowing what shall befall me there, except that the Holy Spirit testifies to me in every city that imprisonments and afflictions await me" (Acts 20:22–23). In the epistle to the Colossians, Paul puts it more boldly: "Now I rejoice in my sufferings for your sake, and in my flesh I complete what is lacking in Christ's afflictions for the sake of his body, that is, the church" (Col. 1:24). Indeed, "I bear on my body the marks *(stigmata)* of Jesus" (Gal. 6:17).

The solidarity of the exalted Son of Man with his own finds eloquent expression in the Matthean parable of the last judgment (Mt. 25:31–46) in which the returning Son of Man says that those who succored or did not succor "the least of these my brethren" did or did not do so "to me."

In the Johannine theology, the individual relationship of believers to Christ is stressed more than the corporate relationship. Yet such images as the vine and its branches (Jn. 15:1f.) express the solidarity of Christ with those who "abide" in him.

Whatever the images employed, the New Testament writers bear witness to the solidarity of the risen Lord with his people. And this has its antecedents in the way in which the earthly Jesus identified himself with his followers before Easter. It finds expression also in the communal pledge of the resurrection appearances. It is the concern of the intercessory prayer of Jesus: "That they may all be one; even as thou, Father, art in me, and I in thee, that they also may be in us, so that the world may believe that thou hast sent me . . . that the love with which thou hast loved me may be in them, and I in them" (Jn. 17:21, 26).

THE CORPORATE NATURE OF RESURRECTION FAITH

This heading is the subtitle of Peter Selby's volume, *Look for the Living.* Resurrection faith, he says,

> is akin to other kinds of communal believing; it rests not merely on what is able to be verified historically but also on the matching which is discernible between the implications contained in the story the church tells and the values by which it lives. Had there been no matching there could have been no faith. . . . What we are looking for are the characteristics of a community which could tell the resurrection story and match it with its life; only such a community could credibly claim that what happened to Jesus contains within it the destiny of mankind.[30]

Indeed. Those first disciples who said, "We have seen the Lord," were credible witnesses because the story of Jesus had become their story.

Luke portrays this by drawing many parallels between his first volume, the Gospel, and his second volume, the Acts. His early description of Jesus as one who increased "in wisdom and in stature, and in favor *(chariti)* with God and man" (Lk. 2:52) is paralleled by his description of the early community which "day by day . . . [was] praising God and having favor *(echontes chariti)* with all the people" (Acts 2:46–47). His first miracle story in the second volume recalls Jesus' raising the lame—and the authorities marveled at the boldness of Peter and John and "recognized that they *had been with Jesus*" (Acts 4:13). Once Peter had strenuously denied this when a servant girl said, "This man also *was with him*" (Lk. 22:56), Now he manifests in word and deed that he was and is a companion of the living Christ. Stephen's prayer for his enemies (Acts 7:60) parallels the prayer of Jesus (Lk. 23:34). When Jesus came to Jerusalem his adversaries said: "He stirs up the people by teaching all over Judaea. He started from Galilee and *now he is here* (Lk. 23:5, Moffatt). When his followers come to Europe their adversaries say, "These men who have turned the world upside down *have come here also*" (Acts 17:6). Communal life gave credence to the communal message: "The whole body of believers was united in heart and soul. Not a man of them claimed any of his possessions as his own, but everything was held in common, while the apostles bore witness with great power to the resurrection of the Lord Jesus" (Acts 4:32–33, NEB).

Using the imagery of Jewish sacrifice, Paul describes the apostolic mission by giving thanks to God "who continually leads us about, captives in Christ's triumphal procession, and everywhere uses us to reveal and spread abroad the fragrance of the knowledge of himself! We are indeed the incense offered by Christ to God, both for those who are on the way to salvation, and for those who are on the way to perdition. . . . When we declare the word we do it in sincerity, as from God and in God's sight, as members of Christ" (2 Cor. 2:14–15, 17, NEB).

With these reminders of the corporate character of the Easter faith we come to the manner in which the resurrection is expressed in the worship and in the service of the church.

THE RESURRECTION AND THE WORSHIP OF THE CHURCH

THE LORD'S DAY

In Chapter II we noted that "the first day of the week," a phrase prominent in the Easter narratives, appears to have liturgical overtones. Our question then was whether liturgical tradition shaped the Easter narratives or whether the Easter history shaped liturgical tradition. Our conclusion was that Easter history provides the origin for "the first day."

Now we are concerned with liturgical tradition.[31] How and when did "the first day of the week" become "the Lord's day"?

Apart from the Easter narratives, the New Testament references are tantalizingly scarce (1 Cor. 16:2; Acts 20:7; Rev. 1:10). We may assume that the earliest Jewish Christian communities in Palestine retained the places and times of Jewish worship. Luke places the gift of the Spirit at the Jewish Feast of Pentecost. We read that "Peter and John were going up to the temple at the hour of prayer, the ninth hour" (Acts 3:1). It would be only natural that the great feasts, such as Passover, were continued, especially when the Passover lent itself so well to the new Pascha in Christ (1 Cor. 5:7f.).

Luke links Paul's missionary witness with Jewish Sabbath meetings: at Perga (Acts 13:14), at Antioch of Pisidia (13:14), at Philippi (16:13), at Thessalonica (17:2), and at Corinth (18:4). Acts implies that Paul observed the Passover before leaving Philippi (20:6) and that he hurried to reach Jerusalem by Pentecost (20:16). Undoubtedly, in the early days of the church there must have been considerable overlapping of Jewish feasts and the new connotations that early Christians gave them.[32]

Yet Christian worship could not simply be a continuation of Jewish worship. Some have suggested that the earliest followers soon began to prolong the Sabbath into the first day of the week. Certainly there was worship and assembly on the first day of the week for the Gentile churches. This became the Lord's Day, the day that celebrated the resurrection.

In the postcanonical literature of the early church we find some references to the first day as the Lord's day. Early in the second century Ignatius writes in his Letter to the Magnesians:

Those, then, who lived by ancient practices arrived at a new hope. [He is referring to prophetic protest against Sabbath abuse, cf. Isa. 1:13f.] They ceased to keep the Sabbath and lived by the Lord's Day, on which our life as well as theirs shone forth, thanks to him and his death. . . . How, then, can we live without him when even the prophets, who were his disciples by the Spirit, awaited him as their teacher? He, then, whom they were rightly expecting, raised them from the dead, when he came [perhaps a reference to Mt. 27:52].[33]

Ignatius clearly links the Lord's Day with Easter.

Two other early Christian documents, whose dates are quite uncertain but may be from 70 to 150, make mention of the day of worship. *The Epistle of Barnabas* says: "Wherefore also we observe the eight day as a time of rejoicing, for on it Jesus both arose from the dead and, when he had appeared, ascended into the heavens" (15:9).[34] *The Didache* includes liturgical instructions: "On every Lord's Day—his special day—come together and break bread and give thanks, first confessing your sins so that your sacrifice may be pure."[35]

It is not until we come to Justin's *First Apology* (ca. 155) that we meet the word "Sunday":

And on the day called Sunday there is a meeting in one place of those who live in cities or the country, and the memoirs of the apostles [probably a Gospel lesson] or the writings of the prophets are read as long as time permits. When the reader has finished, the president in a discourse urges and invites [us] to the imitation of these noble things. Then we all stand up together and offer prayers. And, as said before, when we have finished the prayer, bread is brought, and wine and water, and the president similarly sends up prayers and thanksgivings to the best of his ability, and the congregation assents, saying the Amen; the distribution, and reception of the consecrated [elements] by each one, takes place and they are sent to the absent by the deacons. Those who prosper, and who so wish, contribute, each one as much as he chooses to. . . . We all hold this common gathering on Sunday, since it is the first day, on which God transforming darkness and matter made the universe, and Jesus Christ our Saviour rose from the dead on the same day. For they crucified him on the day before Saturday, and on the day after Saturday, he appeared to his apostles and disciples and taught them these

things which I have passed on to you for your serious consideration (67).[36]

What is explicit in Justin is implicit in the New Testament
references to "the first day of the week." That same note
continues in the hymnody of the Lord's Day. Isaac Watts's
adaptation of Ps. 118 is but one example:

> This is the day the Lord hath made;
> He calls the hours His own;
> Let heaven rejoice, let earth be glad,
> And praise surround the throne.
>
> Today He rose and left the dead,
> And Satan's empire fell;
> Today the saints His triumphs spread,
> And all His wonders tell.

THE WORD OF THE LORD

We have noted the centrality of the resurrection in the
early preaching. But the *kērygma,* the proclamation, is not
only the Word *of* (about) the Lord in the sense that the risen
Lord is the content of the message. It is the Word *of* the Lord
in the sense that it is the risen Lord's own word.

Form criticism of the Gospels has shown how the gospel
tradition is radiated by the Easter light. We think again of
Scott Holland's words: "In the Resurrection it was not only
the Lord who was raised from the dead. His life on earth rose
with Him; it was lifted up into its real light."[37]

Frequently, New Testament scholars have sought to sift
the sayings of Jesus into "authentic" and "inauthentic" sayings—asking whether or not a particular saying goes back to
the pre-Easter Jesus. The concern is legitimate enough—but
it does not go far enough if a conclusion is drawn that the
post-Easter church simply read its own faith back into the
mouth of Jesus. That would make the community more creative than its Lord.

Paul says that from now on "we regard no one from a

human point of view; even though we once regarded Christ from a human point of view [literally, "even if we also knew Christ according to the flesh"], we regard him thus no longer" (2 Cor. 5:16). This does not mean that Paul is indifferent to, or unaware of the traditions about Jesus. It means that the teachings of Jesus were remembered and appropriated not as a past but as a present and living word. It is the risen and living Christ who speaks today.

But how? Later Gnostics relied on so-called Easter revelations through secret sayings which Jesus supposedly gave to his disciples between Easter and Ascension. In the *Pistis Sophia,* a document from the third century, this entailed a period of twelve years of such secret teachings! But this is not the manner in which the risen Lord's Word is heard in the New Testament. Its characteristic literary form is the gospel.

How shall we understand the manner in which the teachings of Jesus were remembered and transmitted? We shall not underestimate the instruction which Jesus himself gave his disciples during his ministry and which was handed down through memorization and oral recital prior to the writing of the four Gospels.[38] But attention must also be given to the role of early Christian prophecy. A recent article by M. E. Boring calls attention to striking similarities between the function of the Spirit-Paraclete as this is described in the Fourth Gospel, and the function of early Christian prophecy.[39] "But the Counselor, the Holy Spirit, whom the Father will send in my name, he will teach you all things, and bring to your remembrance all that I have said to you" (Jn. 14:26). There is good reason to believe that this was also the function of Christian prophets in the early church. "The Paraclete-prophet is an interpreter of the historical Christ event and its historical tradition borne by the community, bringing its meaning home to the present *as the self-interpretation of the risen Christ.*"[40] The Evangelist himself is such a prophet. "Even though the exalted Christ and the historical Jesus blend into each other in John's portrayal, the earthly Jesus and his word are never simply replaced by the word of the exalted Christ, so that John does not sacrifice history to mythology."[41] This is the way in which the Spirit teaches and brings to remembrance. The light of Easter, through the Spirit, makes the gospel genre not "the memoirs of the apostles" (as Justin called the Gospels) but the Easter Lord's own word for the new day.

BAPTISM

There is considerable evidence in the New Testament, especially in the narratives of Acts 18:24 to 19:7, that a continuing movement of John the Baptist's followers made it imperative for the early church to distinguish John's preparatory baptism of repentance from Christian baptism in the name of Jesus. The Gospels indicate that John's baptism pointed forward to the one who would baptize with the Spirit —and Christian baptism, which expresses our incorporation into the crucified and risen Lord, is described as the "seal" of the Spirit. Thus, there is but one Christian baptism: "There is one body and one Spirit, just as you were called to the one hope that belongs to your call, one Lord, one faith, one baptism, one God and Father of us all, who is above all and through all and in all" (Eph. 4:4–6).

In his baptism by John, Jesus had expressed his utter solidarity with sinners. He had joined his people as a penitent and had accepted for himself God's judgment. The best commentary on his own baptism is found in Jesus' words: "Are you able to drink the cup that I drink, or to be baptized with the baptism with which I am baptized?" (Mk. 10:38). In the Old Testament, the "cup" is often the cup of God's judgment (Isa. 51:17). In Jesus' word, "baptism" is a parallel metaphor —being overwhelmed by the deep waters of calamity (Ps. 69:2, 15). In his baptism Jesus identified himself with us. There the road to the cross began.

His baptism led him into the wilderness. As Israel was first designated "God's Son" in the wilderness (Ex. 4:22; Hos. 11:1), so in his baptism Jesus was declared to be God's own beloved Son—and the Voice from heaven was attended by the descent of the Spirit on him. Thus, from the outset of the gospel story, God's promise and presence are to be found in Jesus, a promise and presence fulfilled in his crucifixion and resurrection—through which the bearer of the Spirit becomes the giver of the new life in the Spirit. Christian baptism in the name of Jesus (which in Mt. 28:19 becomes baptism in the threefold name) expresses Easter faith. His life for us is now our life in him.

We shall not consider here all the baptismal images of the New Testament.[42] We simply call attention to those images which are specifically linked with the resurrection of Jesus. We have already had occasion to refer to two passages in Paul's letters:

> Do you not know that all of us who have been baptized into Christ Jesus were baptized into his death? We were buried therefore with him by baptism into death, so that as Christ was raised from the dead by the glory of the Father, we too might walk in newness of life. For if we have been united with him in a death like his, we shall certainly be united with him in a resurrection like his. . . . But if we have died with Christ, we believe that we shall also live with him. For we know that Christ being raised from the dead will never die again; death no longer has dominion over him. The death he died he died to sin, once for all, but the life he lives he lives to God. So you also must consider yourselves dead to sin and alive to God in Christ Jesus. (Rom. 6:3–5, 8–11)

> In him also you were circumcised with a circumcision made without hands, by putting off the body of flesh in the circumcision of Christ [this circumcision of Christ is doubtless to be understood as "the blood of Christ"]; and you were buried with him in baptism, in which you were also raised with him through faith in the working of God, who raised him from the dead. (Col. 2:11–12)

In such passages the "you" is plural, as is the "we." Paul does not forget the corporate character of resurrection faith in baptism. "For as many of you as were baptized into Christ have put on Christ. There is neither Jew nor Greek, there is neither slave nor free, there is neither male nor female; for you are all one in Christ Jesus" (Gal. 3:27–28).

Along with these Pauline passages, we have had occasion also to note a striking passage in The First Epistle of Peter:

> For Christ also died for sins once for all, the righteous for the unrighteous, that he might bring us to God, being put to death in the flesh but made alive in the spirit ["quickened by the Spirit," KJV]; in which he went and preached to the spirits in prison, who formerly did not obey, when God's patience waited in the days of Noah, during the building of the ark, in which a few, that is, eight persons, were saved through water. Baptism, which corresponds to this, now saves you, not as a removal of dirt from the body but as an appeal to God for a clear conscience, through the resurrection of Jesus Christ, who has gone into heaven and is at the right hand of God, with angels, authorities, and powers subject to him. (1 Pet. 3:18–22)

In Chapter II we pointed to this passage as an expression of the "Christus Victor" theme—that there is no nook or cranny in all creation where the saving word of the gospel has not gone. Here we note its reference to baptism. Noah and his few folk were saved, not *from* water (as in the Genesis story), but *through* water. From what were they saved?

Behind this imagery is the Enoch tradition of the intertestamental literature. Enoch, that shadowy figure of Genesis, who walked with God and "was not, for God took him" (Gen. 5:24), in later tradition became the recipient of divine mysteries, privileged to visit the netherworld as well as to approach the divine presence. In his visit to the netherworld he met the fallen angels, the principalities and powers who were the fallen "sons of God" of Gen. 6:4. These implored him to take their petition for clemency to God—but there was no remission of punishment. Since the Enoch literature is clearly alluded to in other New Testament books (even cited in Jude 14), there is every reason to conclude that 1 Pet. 3:18ff. alludes to this tradition in order to contrast Enoch's witness with the effectual "preaching" of the risen Christ to all the principalities and powers of this world.[43]

In view of this larger context we can begin to understand what is meant by the phrase that Noah was saved *through* water. Noah and his family were delivered *through* the water of the flood *from* a demonic environment described in the Genesis myth (Gen. 6:1–4) and interpreted through the Enoch tradition.

And "this water prefigured the water of baptism through which you are now brought to safety. Baptism . . . brings salvation through the resurrection of Jesus Christ" (1 Pet. 3:21, NEB). That is to say, the victory of Christ is signified also in baptism. That is why some baptismal liturgies, both ancient and modern, include a "renunciation" of the devil. In the Western church this appears to have its first expression in *The Apostolic Tradition* of Hippolytus (written about 215 in Rome):

> And when the presbyter takes hold of each one of those who are to be baptized, let him bid him renounce, saying: "I renounce thee, Satan, and all they service and all thy works."

In this liturgy the renunciation is followed by an anointing with the oil of exorcism and the words, "Let all evil spirits depart from thee."[44]

This baptismal imagery may be unfamiliar to many of us. Yet we need not dismiss it as antiquated or magical. It sought to portray dramatically in baptism Easter's victory over evil, and to assure the believers that this victory was for them. It is not far removed from the much more familiar words of Paul: "I am sure that neither death, nor life, nor angels, nor principalities, nor things present, nor things to come, nor powers, . . . nor anything else in all creation, will be able to separate us from the love of God in Christ Jesus our Lord" (Rom. 8:38–39). Finally, it called new Christians to active and costly discipleship. Written in a time when Christians faced difficult decisions, the epistle (as the early liturgies that sought to express its imagery) constituted a summons: "Just as Christ after his death preached to the demonic patrons of the heathen rulers, so Christians ought to preach to the heathen rulers in their communities, even if this brings death to them."[45]

Liturgy *(leitourgia)* is not confined to the cultic liturgy of worship. The liturgy of worship must find expression in the liturgy of service. The word *leitourgia,* although it came to have particular reference to cultic worship, originally expressed any form of public service. It derives from *lēitos* ("of the people," "public") and *ergon* ("work").

THE LORD'S SUPPER

We have noted how yesterday and tomorrow meet in the Lord's Supper. The Supper points back to the night when Jesus was betrayed, and it points forward "until he comes" (1 Cor. 11:23–26). Yesterday and tomorrow meet in our present communion with the Lord. "This is my body . . . my blood."

The "corporate Christ" is present in the Supper. "The cup of blessing which we bless, is it not a participation *(koinōnia)* in the blood of Christ? The bread which we break, is it not a participation *(koinōnia)* in the body of Christ? Because there is one bread, we who are many are one body, for we all partake of the same bread" (1 Cor. 10:16–17). The KJV reads *koinōnia* here as "communion"; the NEB renders it as "a means of sharing." Stuart Currie's study of the word suggested that in Paul's epistles *koinōnia* is best rendered "alliance" or covenant bond.[46] In any event, the Supper expresses our union with Christ and with each other.

This has important implications. Paul was deeply troubled by the lovelessness that characterized the community in Corinth:

> When you meet together, it is not the Lord's supper that you eat. For in eating, each one goes ahead with his own meal, and one is hungry and another is drunk. . . . Whoever, therefore, eats the bread or drinks the cup of the Lord in an unworthy manner will be guilty of profaning *the body and blood of the Lord.* Let a man

examine himself, and so eat of the bread and drink of the cup. For any one who eats and drinks without discerning *the body* eats and drinks judgment upon himself." (1 Cor. 11:20–21, 27–29)

Paul is not speaking about irreverent handling of the elements. He implies that whoever eats and drinks unworthily is like those who originally crucified Jesus, for "the body and blood of the Lord" means "the Lord who was crucified." But in the very next sentence "the body" is the church. Not to discern his body (the church) through loveless attitudes toward its members is as real a profanation of Christ as to reject him outright.

Here, as elsewhere, Jesus Christ cannot be separated from those who are his. We are reminded of Jesus' words: "For whoever is ashamed of me and of my words in this adulterous and sinful generation, of him will the Son of man also be ashamed, when he comes in the glory of his Father with the holy angels" (Mk. 8:38). Because many Greek manuscripts omit "words," the NEB renders this saying: "If anyone is ashamed of me and mine [of me and of my folk, my followers] ..." There is more than one way in which we can be ashamed of the Lord.[47]

That the Lord's Supper celebrates the resurrection as well as remembering and appropriating the passion of Jesus is clear from the Easter narratives in which the risen Lord is known in the breaking of bread (Lk. 24:35). Luke points to this not only in the Emmaus story but also in his description of the forty days in Acts 1:4 (if we read *synalizomenos* as "while eating with them" instead of "while staying with them"). Again, in Acts 2:42, the joyous breaking of bread can be understood in eucharistic terms. And Peter tells Cornelius that the risen Lord manifested himself "to us who were chosen by God as witnesses, who ate and drank with him after he rose from the dead" (Acts 10:41).

Cross and resurrection are inseparable in the New Testament faith. It is not surprising that some New Testament traditions of the Supper (e.g., Luke) stress especially the resurrection side, while others (e.g., Jn. 6:52–59) stress more the death of Christ. Liturgical studies have shown that the former tendency continues in *The Didache*[48] and in the liturgy of Serapion. The latter stress on the passion finds its early expression in the Roman liturgy of Hippolytus and in the liturgies familiar to us. Oscar Cullmann has argued that Paul so combined both motifs that the unity of the Lord's Supper was preserved.[49]

This is not the place to dwell on the bitter theological controversies over the manner of Christ's presence in the Supper. Despite the unhappy differences that made the Lord's Supper a barrier to church union instead of the crowning expression of Christian unity in the churches, we may be grateful that today there is a greater agreement and understanding that lead us to greater intercommunion by the churches.[50]

The Lord's Supper is not simply "the last supper." It is an Easter meal. Neville Clark comments:

> The liturgy of the baptized moves forward through the preaching of the Word to the Supper of the Lord; and in the doing of the eucharist the reality of the Resurrection is bodied forth and the message of the Resurrection is enshrined. . . . In the eucharistic celebration the Church is set between the Christ who has come and the Christ who will come, between the Lord who has risen and the Lord who will appear in glory. The Cross and Resurrection dominate and control.[51]

The "third day" and the "last day" meet in "the Lord's day" in the worship of the church.

THE RESURRECTION AND THE SERVICE OF THE CHURCH

The *leitourgia* of worship leads to the church's service in the world. Luke describes a new chapter in the church's mission with these words: "While they were worshiping *(lei-*

tourgountōn) the Lord and fasting, the Holy Spirit said, 'Set apart for me Barnabas and Saul for the work to which I have called them.' Then after fasting and praying they laid their hands on them and sent them off' (Acts 13:2–3). The Spirit who sends them is "the Spirit of Jesus" (Acts 16:7). The Lord who is present in the liturgy of worship goes with them in the liturgy of service in the world.

HERALDING EASTER IN THE WORLD

We may begin with the closing scene in Matthew. The disciples have gone to Galilee, to the mountain to which Jesus had directed them. "And when they saw him they worshiped him" (Mt. 28:17). Matthew does not idealize the scene. Even in their worship "some doubted." But Jesus came to them—including those who doubted (cf. Lk. 24: 37,41; Jn. 20:24–29). He came to them and assured them that all authority in heaven and on earth has been given to him. He sends them into the world to make disciples of all nations, baptizing and teaching, and assures them that he is with them to the close of the age. The Lord is Emmanuel, God with us (Mt. 1:23). He is with them in worship: "For where two or three are gathered in my name, there am I in the midst of them" (18:20). He is with them in mission: "And lo, I am with you always, to the close of the age" (28:20).

We have noted that Luke's ascension narrative portrays a going away. Van Stempvoort[52] has suggested that Luke gives us two interpretations of the ascension. The first finds expression in the closing verses of Luke's Gospel. Here worship is the setting:

> Then he led them out as far as Bethany, and lifting up his hands he blessed them. While he blessed them, he parted from them, and was carried up into heaven. And they worshiped him, and returned to Jerusalem with great joy, and were continually in the temple blessing God. (Lk. 24:50–53)[53]

We may note that Luke's Gospel had begun with a scene in the Temple in which a priest was not able to bless the people, so that his *leitourgia* (Lk. 1:23) was an unfinished liturgy. Luke's first interpretation of the ascension suggests a completed liturgy in which the Easter Lord blesses his followers. It is not a long step for the author of Hebrews to develop this theme by portraying Jesus as the great high priest who now carries on his *leitourgia* (Heb. 8:6) in the heavenly sanctuary. Luke's first narrative portrays the ascension in terms of doxology.

However, as van Stempvoort goes on, to see the ascension only as the climax of Easter worship would confine it to the gathered church. That would allow the church to forget the world mission. Luke does not forget the mission. In his second narrative interpretation (Acts 1:6–11), the ascension is a call to mission. "It is not for you to know times or seasons. . . . But you shall receive power when the Holy Spirit has come upon you; and you shall be my witnesses in Jerusalem and in all Judea and Samaria and to the end of the earth." With these words, "as they were looking on, he was lifted up, and a cloud took him out of their sight."

The disciples are called back to the present. "Men of Galilee, why do you stand looking into heaven?" They will not reach the future by speculating about "times or seasons" or by "gazing into heaven." They are called to serve their Lord in the present, with marching orders instead of blueprints. So to interpret the ascension narrative is to see that the ascension of Jesus is into heaven—and into all the world. Luke's second interpretation is not doxological but missional.

How can we relate Luke's "going away" to Matthew's "I am with you always"? Paul Minear suggests:

> One answer to this question is suggested by parables and anecdotes in the Synoptic Gospels. The Lord, being present with his disciples, gives them tasks to accomplish. Then he journeys into a far country. Or he sends them out into the villages of Israel to

continue and to extend his ministry, with the assurance that he will come to them. The fact of the task presupposes that Jesus has been with them; it presupposes that in one sense (in the task itself) he accompanies them. But in another sense the departs from his disciples for the period of their work. . . . His presence is necessary in assigning servants their posts. But his absence is also necessary if their freedom and their responsibility are to be safeguarded. The testing of their faith requires his absence, for their patience and fidelity cannot be gauged unless he leaves them for what seems to them too long a period. . . . His absence is for their sake (Jn. 16). . . . Yet he remains present in the task itself.[54]

In this connection, Hans Werner Bartsch[55] has suggested that one reason why the ascension often seems to us to be no more than a fairy tale is that we have expressed its meaning too exclusively in the pageantry of triumph instead of seeing it as the end of the Easter appearances. Can we imagine, he asks, what a shock this posed for the disciples? They had expected their Lord here and now to establish his kingdom on earth—and instead he went away! We ought to understand this shock, he goes on, for our faith has been jolted time and again by hopes disappointed in a world that shows so little outward evidence of the risen Lord. It is easier to see the crucified Christ in history than the risen Christ.[56] But the ascension shows us how sober was apostolic faith. Those first followers had to meet the world as it was. Seen in this light, the ascension is the "nevertheless" of faith. Here Easter faith was put to the test—and it must meet each recurring test with the same trust.

Withal, the ascension narrative is linked with all the Easter appearances in emphasizing that the risen Lord only meets his followers to call them to service. Men and women cannot meet the Lord of Easter without becoming his messengers.

Easter summons the church to Christ's mission in the world. His Spirit attends them for this apostolic vocation. Only so is Jesus' prayer fulfilled:

As thou didst send *(apesteilas)* me into the world, so I have sent *(apesteila)* them into the world. And for their sake I consecrate myself, that they also may be consecrated in truth. I do not pray for these only, but also for those who believe in me through their word, that they may be one; even as thou, Father, art in me, and I in thee, that they also may be in us, so that the world may believe that thou hast sent me . . . so that the world may know that thou hast sent me and hast loved them even as thou hast loved me. (Jn. 17:18–21, 23)

What do the words "that the world may believe" and "that the world may know" imply? Frequently they have been taken to suggest that the world will accept Jesus. In the later chapters of John's Gospel, however, "the world" or "this world" has a negative connotation—and in this prayer we need to note that Jesus says, "I am not praying for the world" (17:9). Of course, "God so loved the world that he gave his only Son . . . not to condemn the world, but that the world might be saved through him" (3:16–17). But John has no illusions about "the world" that hates God's truth and so will hate Jesus' followers as it had hated him.

Evangelism is inseparable from the church's mission, but the mission is measured not by statistics but by faithful discipleship. Kierkegaard wrote: "So long as this world lasts and the Christian Church within it, it is a militant Church, yet it has the promise that the gates of hell shall not prevail against it. But woe, woe to the Christian Church if it would triumph in this world, for then it is not the Church that triumphs, but the world has triumphed."[57] One of the "horizons of Christian community" (to use the title of one of Minear's books) is "the frontier of God's warfare against evil."[58] We recall that Jesus said, "Do not think that I have come to bring peace on earth; I have not come to bring peace, but a sword" (Mt. 10:34). That sword is "the sword of the Spirit, which is the word of God" (Eph. 6:17).

We have seen the resurrection of Jesus as the vindication of God's righteousness. The church of the risen Christ cannot be aloof from the issues of justice and freedom. Paul says that "the rulers of this age," the principalities and powers, did not know what they were doing when they crucified the Lord of glory (1 Cor. 2:8), for the victim of injustice became the victor. The church of the risen Christ shares in its Lord's continuing battle "until he has put all his enemies under his feet" (1 Cor. 15:25). The principalities and powers find contemporary expression in the structures of this world that make for hunger and injustice and bondage.[59] That is the church's business also. We may not "be conformed to this world" (Rom. 12:2). We "are not contending against flesh and blood, but against the principalities, against the powers, against the world rulers of this present darkness, against the spiritual hosts of wickedness in the heavenly places" (Eph. 6:12).

Accordingly, evangelism and social action cannot be alternatives for the church of the risen Lord. "Truly, I say to you, as you did it not to one of the least of these [the hungry, the lonely, the exploited, the oppressed], you did it not to me" (Mt. 25:45). One of Christ's gallant warriors in our century was G. A. Studdert-Kennedy, whose wartime witness as "Woodbine Willie" found later expression in an unrelenting concern for the disinherited of industrial society. He knew what it meant to be on the frontier of God's warfare:

> Peace does not mean the end of all our striving,
>   Joy does not mean the drying of our tears;
> Peace is the power that comes to souls arriving
>   Up to the light where God Himself appears.
>
> Joy is the wine that God is ever pouring
>   Into the hearts of those who strive with Him,
> Light'ning their eyes to vision and adoring,
>   Strength'ning their arms to warfare glad and grim.
>
> . . . .
> Bread of Thy Body give me for my fighting,
>   Give me to drink Thy Sacred Blood for wine,
> While there are wrongs that need me for the righting,
>   While there is warfare splendid and divine.

> Give me for light, the sunshine of Thy sorrow,
> Give me for shelter the shadow of Thy Cross,
> Give me to share the glory of Thy morrow,
> Gone from my heart the bitterness of Loss.[60]
> —G. A. Studdert-Kennedy,
> "The Suffering God"

(From *The Unutterable Beauty: Collected Poetry,* by G. A. Studdert-Kennedy; Hodder & Stoughton, Ltd., 1927. Reprinted by permission of Hodder & Stoughton Ltd.)

So we come back to Jesus' prayer and ask what it means "that the world may believe that thou hast sent me" and "that the world may know that thou hast sent me." These statements, as Raymond Brown puts it, "do not mean that the world will accept Jesus; rather the Christian believers will offer to the world the same type of challenge that Jesus offered—a challenge to recognize God in Jesus." The life of the Christian community gives the world another chance because it "provokes the world to self-judgment."[61]

What does this mean?

DEMONSTRATING EASTER TO THE WORLD

In the Johannine prayer, the life of the Christian community, expressed in love and unity, will bring the world to self-judgment.

In the epistle to the Ephesians this is seen in the broken wall of hostility that once stood between Jew and Gentile. In the church the mystery of God's purpose is to be evident. "And he came and preached peace to you who were far off and peace to those who were near; for through him we both have access in one Spirit to the Father" (Eph. 2:17–18). This brings the apostle to a crowning expression of apostolic vocation:

> To me, though I am the very least of all the saints, this grace was given, to preach to the Gentiles the unsearchable riches of Christ, and to make all [if *pantas,* "humankind," belongs in the

text] see what is the plan of the mystery hidden for ages in God who created all things; that through the church the manifold wisdom of God might now be made known to the principalities and powers in the heavenly places. (Eph. 3:8–10)

Paul Minear has called attention to the triple audience of the apostolic vocation. First is the audience of the Gentiles. Paul himself had to pay the price of his calling in breaching this wall of hostility. He is "a prisoner for Christ Jesus on behalf of you Gentiles" (Eph. 3:1). The second audience is all of humankind. Doubtless Paul means the one humanity to which Jews and Gentiles belonged. The third audience is composed of the principalities and powers. The church must make known to the "world rulers" the mystery of God's purpose in Christ. "Although they may be located in heavenly places, their work may be observed in the sons of disobedience, those who live by the passions of the flesh and are dead through their sinful behavior (2:1–3). Their earthly sons as 'children of wrath' betray the character of their parents (2:3)."[62] Can the structures of prejudice and division see God's purpose in the community called church? Is the church's message of the resurrection matched by the church's life? Can the world see in the church the firstfruits of God's new creation?

In other words, the story which the church tells of the crucified and risen Christ is credible only if the church's story is matched by the church's life. Without such demonstration, the church's mission of evangelism will simply erect another wall of hostility, an arrogant and divisive wall between "us" and "them." Long ago, Jonathan Swift satirized such presumption in scathing lines:

> We are God's chosen few,
>   All others will be damned;
> There is no place in heaven for you,
>   We can't have heaven crammed![63]

In Minear's words, "The internal growth of the new community into the measure of the stature of the fullness of Christ

... constituted the announcement of the coming destruction of all other dividing walls between nations, races, classes, sexes." Ephesians presents this as "the essential vocation of the church."[64]

SERVICE IN HOPE

In various ways the New Testament describes the vocation of the church, expressed both in its life and in its outreach, as a vocation shaped by hope in the future of Jesus Christ. For example, Paul's chapter on Christian responsibilities and conduct within the orders of this world (Romans 13) closes with a reminder of "what hour it is," for "the night is far gone, the day is at hand" (Rom. 13:11–12).

The Great Commission, with which Matthew closes, has an echo in Matthew's version of the apocalyptic discourse of Jesus: "And this gospel of the kingdom will be preached throughout the whole world, as a testimony to all nations; and then the end will come" (Mt. 24:14).

In the apocalyptic panorama of 2 Thess. 2:6–7, we read of a final rebellion of lawlessness—but we also read "of the restraining hand which ensures that he [the ultimate adversary] shall be revealed only at the proper time. For already the secret power of wickedness is at work, secret only for the present until the Restrainer disappears from the scene" (NEB). Who or what is this restraining power? Some commentators take this to be the restraining order of the Roman Empire. Others, more plausibly, see in the restraining hand the power of the gospel message which will be preached until the end.[65]

In the Apocalypse, the vision of the four horsemen fits this latter interpretation. To be sure, most commentators put these four together so that all four are sinister foes—invasion, civil war, famine, and death. Yet the first is unlike the others. "And I saw, and behold, a white horse, and its rider had a bow; and a crown was given to him, and he went out conquering and to conquer" (Rev. 6:2). White is not a color for evil in this book. Who is this rider? Some have wanted to identify him with the victorious Christ who rides on a white horse (19:11) for the last decisive battle with evil. But that is hardly possible, for the Lamb (Christ) opens the seal that brings the first horseman on the scene. Who is he? Does this first horseman not portray the march of the gospel? In this first unveiling of the future, John not only sees the dread figures of war, famine, and death; he also sees the proclamation of the gospel as a decisive factor in world history. John's vision parallels the Matthean reminder that the gospel of the kingdom will be preached throughout the whole world, and then the end will come.[66]

Such portrayals do not encourage any "triumphalism" on the part of the church. The servant church is not greater than its Servant Lord. In Paul's words:

> Therefore, having this ministry *(diakonia)* by the mercy of God, we do not lose heart. . . . We are afflicted in every way, but not crushed; perplexed, but not driven to despair; persecuted, but not forsaken; struck down, but not destroyed; always carrying in the body the death of Jesus, so that the life of Jesus may also be manifested in our bodies. For while we live we are always being given up to death for Jesus' sake, so that the life of Jesus may be manifested in our mortal flesh. So death is at work in us, but life in you. (2 Cor. 4:1, 8–11)

The church which tells the story of the crucified and risen Jesus is credible when its story is matched by its life. "And he died for all, that those who live might live no longer for themselves but for him who for their sake died and was raised" (2 Cor. 5:15).

Easter's past and Easter's future meet in Easter's meaning for the present—for the living of these days.

V

Appropriating
the Message
of the Resurrection

The New Testament message of the resurrection is indeed the "many-splendoured" disclosure of God's deed in Christ. We have described its significance as a past event, its promise of the future, and have seen how memory and hope shape its meaning for today.

Is this sequence of exposition integral to the New Testament? If so, what are some implications for our own personal appropriation of the Easter message?

One way in which to assess the sequence of our exposition is to consider the triad of "faith, hope, love" (1 Cor. 13:13) in Pauline theology. Stuart Currie began his study of this triad with the words: "The distinctive gems of the biblical treasure are often shown to best advantage not in isolation but in an arrangement which displays their singular faceted beauty."[1]

This triad is not confined to a single passage. For example, Paul thanks God for those in Thessalonica, "remembering before our God and Father your work of faith and labor of love and steadfastness of hope in our Lord Jesus Christ" (1 Thess. 1:3). Similarly, he thanks God for those in Colossae "because we have heard of your faith in Christ Jesus and of the love which you have for all the saints, because of the hope laid up for you in heaven" (Col. 1:4–5).

While faith, hope, and love are inseparably linked together, as Currie reminded us, one member of the triad may receive special emphasis when Paul is addressing particular situations. In 1 Cor. 13:13, love receives this emphasis because Corinthian individualism and enthusiasm needs this reminder most: "So faith, hope, *love* abide, these three; but the greatest of these is *love.*" In Gal. 5:1–6, faith receives the emphasis because the Galatians are in danger of losing the righteousness of faith in a legalistic devotion to the law: "For through the Spirit, by *faith,* we wait for the hope of righteousness, . . . *faith* working through love." In Rom. 5:1–5, hope receives special stress. The illustration of Abraham (in Romans 4) has shown that "faith can grasp what it can hardly hang on to, envision what it can barely expect, take in as promise what seems impossible of fulfilment."[2] So Romans 5 begins: "Therefore, since we are justified by faith, we have peace with God through our Lord Jesus Christ . . . and we rejoice in our *hope* of sharing the glory of God. More than that, we rejoice in our sufferings, knowing that suffering produces endurance, and endurance produces character, and character produces *hope,* and *hope* does not disappoint us, because God's love has been poured into our hearts."

Paul's earliest letter is the First Epistle to the Thessalonians. Here the triad not only appears in the opening thanksgiving but inheres in the very structure of the epistle. At the close of the first chapter Paul uses a missionary formula (not unlike the pattern that Luke elaborates in Paul's address at Athens in Acts 17): "How you turned to God from idols, to serve a living and true God, and to wait for his Son from heaven, whom he raised from the dead, Jesus who delivers us from the wrath to come" (1 Thess. 1:9–10). Paul adds that he had sent Timothy "to establish you in your faith" (3:2), so "that I might know your faith" (3:5). Timothy has brought "the good news of your faith and love" (3:6). This section of the epistle closes with a hope-filled prayer: "Now may our God and Father himself, and our Lord Jesus, direct our way to you; and may the Lord make you increase and abound in love to one another and to all men, as we do to you, so that he may establish your hearts unblamable in holiness before our God and Father, at the coming of our Lord Jesus with all his saints" (3:11-13).

With this expression of Christian hope the apostle begins the ethical injunctions of 4:1 to 5:22, a section that closes again: "May the God of peace himself sanctify you wholly; and may your spirit and soul and body be kept sound and blameless at the coming of our Lord Jesus Christ" (5:23).

What is noteworthy in this section of ethical injunctions is that Paul interrupts the ethical discussion with a little apocalypse of Christian hope (4:13 to 5:11), twice reminding his readers that hope governs the present by its encouragement (4:18; 5:11). That is to say, Christian life in the present is bounded by what God has done in raising Jesus from the dead (1:10) and by hope in the coming of him whom God has raised from the dead. Thus, "to serve the living and true God" finds its expression in an ethic through which Christians may "increase and abound in love one to another and to all" and may "encourage one another and build one another up." Paul often reminds us that "love builds up" (1 Cor. 8:1; 10:23).

Thus, faith in what God has done in raising Jesus, and hope in the future of this Jesus whom God raised from the dead, make possible the new life in Christ, a life of love and service. In Moltmann's words: "Faith binds man to Christ. Hope sets this faith open to the comprehensive future of Christ. Hope is therefore the 'inseparable companion' of faith. . . . Thus it is that faith in Christ gives hope its assurance. Thus it is that hope gives faith in Christ its breadth and leads it into life."[3]

We turn now to Paul's most eloquent and familiar words: "So faith, hope, love abide, these three; but the greatest of these is love" (1 Cor. 13:13).

Some interpreters, notably John Calvin,[4] have taken this to mean that faith and hope are limited to this present life, while love endures to eternity. However, the text does not support such a reading. All three—faith, hope, love—abide, in contrast to those gifts of the Spirit which Paul says will pass away.

In a little volume entitled *Faith, Hope, and Love,* Emil Brunner reflected on the implications of this triad. We live, he said, in the three dimensions of time—in the past by memory, in the future by expectation, and in the problematical present:

> Since this is true of human life as such—that we live in the past, in the future, and in the present—we must now ask how we, as Christians, live in the past, in the future, and in the present, and that means how our relation to Jesus Christ affects our living in the past, in the future, and the present. The answer of the New Testament is precisely these three words: we live in the past by faith; we live in the future by hope; and we live in the present by love. That is the reason why each of these great words expresses the whole of our existence without competing with the others. If Saint Paul says, "Love is the greatest of these," this does not mean a difference of greater or lesser importance. All are equally essential and total, because each expresses the relation to Jesus in a particular dimension of time.[5]

While Brunner does not link his discussion specifically to the resurrection, his comments are relevant to our study of the Easter message.

For example, let us turn again to Paul's chapter on the resurrection (1 Corinthians 15). Paul begins with the creedal stress on the resurrection of Jesus as an event in the past. Faith is anchored in this past—"unless you believed in vain." In Brunner's words: "This reconciliation in Jesus Christ—if it is really that—cannot take place more than once. If God really has reconciled the world to himself in Christ, he does not do it again. He has done it, for all time."[6] In Paul's words, "If Christ has not been raised, your faith is futile and you are still in your sins" (15:17). Christ's past has changed our past —which is our guilt. We have to "carry" our past into the present unless God in Christ has taken our past into himself. And this he has done.

Faith leads to hope. The whole of 1 Corinthians 15 illustrates how the resurrection of Jesus is our hope. The chapter closes with the joyous affirmation: "Death is swallowed up in victory. . . . Thanks be to God, who gives us the victory through our Lord Jesus Christ" (15:54, 57). And faith and hope find their expression in loving service: "Therefore, my beloved brethren, be steadfast, immovable, always abounding in the work of the Lord, knowing that in the Lord your labor is not in vain" (15:58).

Without rehearsing our exposition of these dimensions of the Easter message, we draw a few implications for personal appropriation in terms of these dimensions.

FAITH: EASTER AS A GIVEN PAST

Earlier, we criticized interpretations of the Easter message that tend to dismiss the question of its facticity as a given past by approaching the Easter narratives only for what they say about disciples coming to faith. This shifts the reality of the resurrection from something that happened to the crucified Jesus to something that happens to his followers. But we have seen that the New Testament witnesses not only say, "I am certain"; they say, "It is certain."[7] This has important implications for personal faith.

Of course, there is no faith without experience. Yet faith dare not rely simply on subjective experience. It is not enough to sing:

> You ask me how I know He lives:
> He lives within my heart.[8]

Biblical faith is more than faith in one's own faith. Such faith, we all know, is fragile and often fleeting. Like the man who came to Jesus, we often find ourselves saying, "I believe; help my unbelief!" (Mk. 9:24). Should we pretend it is not so?

The New Testament does not pretend. All the Easter narratives portray doubt as well as faith. In the abrupt close of Mark's Gospel, we read that the women fled from the tomb, "for trembling and astonishment had come upon them; and they said nothing to any one, for they were afraid" (Mk. 16:8). Karl Barth comments: "Little wonder that human language begins to stammer at this point even in the New Testament." At the grave, he goes on, only the angels can say "He is risen."[9]

In Matthew's closing scene: "And when they saw him they worshiped him; but some doubted" (Mt. 28:17). Those last three words are not an intrusion; they are part of the story, the good news, that Jesus Christ comes even to disciples who doubt.

In Luke's Easter chapter, Peter ran to the tomb but "went home wondering at what had happened" (Lk. 24:12). The two disciples on the road do not recognize the Christ who meets them. On Easter evening, despite the glad tidings, doubt is still present. When Jesus appeared, "they were startled and frightened, and supposed that they saw a spirit. And he said to them, 'Why are you troubled, and why do questionings rise in your hearts?' " (Lk. 24:37–38). Even then, "they still disbelieved for joy" (24:41).

It is not different in the Fourth Gospel. The beloved disciple may believe at the tomb, but Peter does not (Jn. 20:5). Mary Magdalene mistakes the risen Christ for the gardener (20:15). Disciple doubts are focused in Thomas (20:25). All these Gospel reminders make plain that faith must rest on something more solid than our own feelings.

Faith must have a stronger basis than our fragile experience. What happens when one experiences some dark night of the soul—when God seems far away and when one does not sense the presence of the living Christ? For it can happen.

Here the psalms are our best guide. The psalmist does not pretend to be sure when he is not sure. He knows what it means to experience the "absence" of God:

> I cry aloud to God,
>   aloud to God, that he may hear me.
> In the day of my trouble I seek the Lord;
>   in the night my hand is stretched out without wearying;

> my soul refuses to be comforted.
> I think of God, and I moan;
>> I meditate, and my spirit faints. (Ps. 77:1–3)

The psalmist did not find his faith restored by communing with his own heart. He found faith's certainty by recalling God's redemptive acts in history:

> I will call to mind the deeds of the Lord;
>> yea, I will remember thy wonders of old.
> I will meditate on all thy work,
>> and muse on thy mighty deeds. . . .
>
> Thou art the God who workest wonders,
>> who hast manifested thy might among the peoples.
> Thou didst with thy arm redeem thy people,
>> the sons of Jacob and Joseph. (Ps. 77:11–12, 14–15)

For us those mighty deeds of God are supremely the cross and resurrection of Jesus Christ. Those deeds precede and transcend any deed of our own. That is why the Christian creed does not begin with our experience but with God's deeds in Christ:

> This is the good news which we received, in which we stand, and by which we are saved: that Christ died for our sins according to the Scriptures, that he was buried, that he was raised on the third day; and that he appeared to Peter, then to the Twelve and to many faithful witnesses.
>
> We believe he is the Christ, the Son of the living God. He is the first and the last, the beginning and the end, he is our Lord and our God. Amen.[10]

Faith is faith in God—not faith in the stability and strength of our own faith. "The saying is sure," says a New Testament formula, "If we are faithless, he remains faithful—for he cannot deny himself" (2 Tim. 2:11–13).

That is why we need each other. Personal faith is not a rugged individualism. In his *Life Together,* Dietrich Bonhoeffer said: "The Christian needs another Christian who speaks God's word to him. He needs him again and again when he becomes uncertain and discouraged, for by himself he cannot help himself without belying the truth. He needs his brother man as a bearer and proclaimer of the divine word of salvation. He needs his brother solely because of Jesus Christ. The Christ in his own heart is weaker than the Christ in the word of his brother; his own heart is uncertain, his brother's is sure."[11]

Perhaps that is the way to understand the place of the beloved disciple in the Fourth Gospel. At the supper, Peter had turned to him for understanding (Jn. 13:24). At Easter, the beloved disciple believes when Peter is not yet able to do so (20:5). In the epilogue, the risen Lord appears while "yet the disciples did not know that it was Jesus" (21:4). It is the beloved disciple who says to Peter, "It is the Lord!" (21:7). "When Simon Peter heard that it was the Lord, he . . . sprang into the sea" (21:7), and the other disciples respond by bringing the boat to shore.

We need one another—even, sometimes especially—in our response to the gospel of the resurrection. One's own faith frequently falters. We need one another. Indeed, we are often called to believe and to worship for others when they cannot seem to do so. Even in some dark night of the soul, a person is not alone.

Peter will become a strong leader and spokesman for the apostolic band. But, on that last night, Jesus had said to him: "Simon, Simon, behold, Satan demanded to have you [plural "you"—all of you disciples], that he might sift you [plural "you"] like wheat, but I have prayed for you [singular "you" —for you in particular, Simon] that your faith may not fail; and when you [singular "you"] have turned again, strengthen your brethren" (Lk. 22:31–32).

HOPE: EASTER'S PROMISE

Hope is "the inseparable companion of faith." In The Epistle to the Hebrews, hope is so closely linked to faith that faith is sometimes described as hope. "Now faith is the reality *(hypostasis)* of things hoped for, the proving *(elenchos)* of things not seen" (Heb. 11:1). Studies have shown that Luther's rendering of *hypostasis* as "assurance" introduced a new and untenable meaning into the text by viewing faith as a subjective conviction.[12] The whole chapter illustrates the verse by portraying those who "all died in faith [i.e., in believing hope], not having received what was promised, but having seen it, and greeted it from afar" (11:13). In another place the writer says: "Let us hold fast the confession of our hope without wavering, for he who promised is faithful" (10:23). Where we might have expected to meet the phrase "the confession of our faith," the writer speaks of "the confession of our hope."

We have seen that Easter discloses the future as the future of Jesus Christ and of God's purpose in him. This is far more than an individualistic hope of "what will happen to me," even when it comes to our own hope of resurrection.

In the year 1917, Walter Rauschenbusch, the pioneer of the social gospel, wrote *A Theology for the Social Gospel.* He criticized the individualism of evangelical religion in his day with these words:

> Our personal eschatology is characterized by an unsocial individualism. In the present life we are bound up with wife and children, with friends and work-mates, in a warm organism of complex life. When we die, we join—what? A throng of souls, an unorganized crowd of saints, who each carry a harp and have not even formed an orchestra.[13]

Rauschenbusch's theology is far from satisfying. His volume includes only two passing references to the resurrection of Jesus because the older liberalism which he reflects sought a sufficient basis for Christian faith in the enduring influence of the personality of Jesus. Nonetheless, his protest against a self-centered individualism was a needed correction. Writing from a very different theological perspective, Brunner made the same reminder:

A Christian cannot lead a merely private life; he is committed to the work of God in the world; he takes part in God's world plan. He is not concerned primarily about his own salvation; he is concerned about God's concern, which is for the world. His hope therefore must be both personal and universal.[14]

We may contrast to the individualistic preoccupation which Rauschenbusch criticized a very different vision of the future in the Apocalypse:

Then I looked, and lo, on Mount Zion stood the Lamb, and with him a hundred and forty-four thousand who had his name and his Father's name written on their foreheads. And I heard a voice from heaven like the sound of many waters and like the sound of loud thunder; the voice I heard was like the sound of harpers playing on their harps, and they sing a new song before the throne.... It is these who follow the Lamb wherever he goes; these have been redeemed from mankind as first fruits for God and the Lamb. (Rev. 14:1–4)

John's vision of the hundred and forty-four thousand merges with a vision of "a great multitude which no man could number, from all tribes and peoples and tongues" (Rev. 7:9). Such a vision is both social and universal—yet it is also deeply personal, for that host is not a collective conglomerate. Each person is a person in company with others in that symphony of the redeemed, for each has the name of the Lamb and his Father's name written on the forehead.

That kind of hope finds expression in a passionate concern for God's world. As William Temple said about Studdert-Kennedy: "Salvation was always social. A man might be damned alone; indeed, to be spiritually alone would be damnation. But he could not be saved alone. For to be saved is to be held in the fellowship of Love; the fellowship is part of it."[15] In his letter to the Corinthians, Paul quotes a saying: "What no eye has seen, nor ear heard, nor the heart of man conceived, what God has prepared for those who love him" (1 Cor. 2:9). Love is the touchstone of Christian faith as it is of Christian hope.

LOVE: EASTER LIFE TODAY

"So faith, hope, love abide, these three; but the greatest of these is love." Faith and hope find their expression in love. Paul adds, "Make love your aim" (1 Cor. 14:1)—"strive for love," "zealously follow love."

Love, Jesus had said, is that on which all the law and the prophets depend—love of God and love of neighbor (Mt. 22:34–40). Love, says Paul, is the fulfilling of the law (Gal. 5:14). Love is the "new" commandment because the love of Christ has made it new (Jn. 13:34; 15:12; 1 Jn. 2:7–11). We do not need to demonstrate the primacy of love in New Testament descriptions of the Christian life.

Instead, we may close by returning to the last resurrection appearance narrated in the Gospels (John 21). We are not concerned now to link the narrative to Easter's past. We are not concerned now with Peter's place in the apostolate and the validating of the church's mission. Nor are we examining the history of the Easter traditions reflected in the structure and style of the chapter. We turn to the narrative for what it says to our own response to the Easter message today.

Our exposition of the Easter message has left many questions unanswered. It is not amiss to note that the Johannine chapter begins with disciple questions and uncertainty. Uncertainty made them restless. "I am going fishing," Peter said. "We will go with you," the others said. But the night was fruitless labor and they found no satisfaction in the life they had known before Jesus called them to discipleship.

Then, says the Gospel, as the dawn was breaking, Jesus appeared—but they did not at once recognize him. The meeting becomes a meal—and it is hard not to sense a eucharistic connotation as Jesus "came and took the bread and gave it to them."

The scene soon focuses on Peter and his Lord. Communion with Christ is always a deeply personal experience. Peter sums up all the lights and shadows of our own discipleship —one moment a rock of faith, the next moment unstable and faltering in his loyalty. We may assume that Peter has been having a bad time of it lately, haunted as he is by painful memories of denial. But in this repast with his Lord, Peter finds that the Lord has not forsaken him. Three times he had denied. Three times he may now plight his love.

Peter has many questions to ask his Lord. Who has not? All the disciples, as the various gospel traditions indicate, had questions enough: "Lord, when shall these things be?" "Lord, show us the way." "Lord, will you at this time restore the kingdom to Israel?"

Disciples need not stifle their questions. It would be a shallow faith that has no questions. And yet, disciples need something more than answers to their questions. Peter soon discovers that Christ has not met him here to satisfy his questions about the future—but to ask him a question of his own.

That question is primary and fundamental: "Simon, son of John, do you love me?" Peter had failed in Jerusalem, not because he had not had enough answers to his questions. He had failed because he had not adequately answered the question of his Lord. "Simon, son of John, do you love me?"

Once Peter had answered confidently: "Lord, why cannot I follow you now? I will lay down my life for you" (Jn. 13:37–38). According to Mark, Peter had been supremely confident that he could love "more than these": "Even though they all fall away, I will not. . . . If I must die with you, I will not deny you" (Mk. 14:29, 31).

Not now. A chastened Peter replies: "Lord, you know that I love you. . . . Lord, you know everything, you know that I love you."

> Lord, it is my chief complaint
> That my love is weak and faint;
> Yet I love Thee, and adore:
> O for grace to love Thee more.

How is love expressed? What does love demand? Jesus replies with a charge: "Feed my sheep." Of course, that charge has particular reference to Peter's pastoral office in the church. But the charge "Feed my sheep" has implications for every disciple. Certainly, the last word is not only for Peter but for us all: "Follow me."

The scene is not quite finished. Peter has received his marching orders—but he still wants blueprints. His own questions are beginning to crowd out the question of his Lord. "Peter turned and saw following them the disciple whom Jesus loved. . . . When Peter saw him, he said to Jesus, 'Lord, what about this man?' "

The reply is blunt and brusque. "What is that to you?" Your path is plain. "Follow me." Thomas à Kempis paraphrased this reply: "My son, be not curious, nor trouble thyself with idle anxieties. What is this or that to thee? *follow thou Me.* For what is it to thee, whether that man be such or such, or whether this man do or speak this or that? Thou shalt not need to answer for others, but shalt give account for thyself."[16]

Easter faith leaves us with many questions. But Easter's reality is the person of Jesus Christ. Our response to Easter's Lord is the measure of our response to the gospel.

Notes
and Indexes

Notes

Chapter I. Approaching the Message of the Resurrection

1. Cf. Christopher F. Evans, *Resurrection and the New Testament,* Studies in Biblical Theology, 2d series, No. 12 (London: SCM Press, 1970), pp. 1f.

2. B. Klappert, *Diskussion um Kreuz und Auferstehung* (Wuppertal: Aussaat Verlag, 1968), pp. 9–52.

3. Gerald O'Collins, *What Are They Saying About the Resurrection?* (Paulist Press, 1978), Ch. 1. Cf. also Gerald O'Collins, *The Resurrection of Jesus Christ* (Judson Press, 1973). This was published also as *The Easter Jesus* (London: Darton, Longman & Todd, 1973).

4. O'Collins, *What Are They Saying About the Resurrection?* p. 8.

5. Both Klappert and O'Collins point to Gerhard Ebeling as typical of this view.

6. E.g., O'Collins, *What Are They Saying About the Resurrection?* and Peter Selby, *Look for the Living: The Corporate Nature of Resurrection Faith* (Philadelphia: Fortress Press, 1976; London: SCM Press, 1976). For a critical assessment of recent scholarship, John Alsup, *The Post-Resurrection Appearance Stories of the Gospel Tradition* (Stuttgart: Calwer-Verlag, 1975), Ch. 1. Cf. also C. F. D. Moule, ed., *The Significance of the Message of the Resurrection for Faith in Jesus Christ* (London: SCM Press, 1970).

7. For a brief summary of the kinds of early Easter confessions, cf. Leonhard Goppelt, "The Easter Kerygma in the New Testament," in *The Easter Message Today* (Thomas Nelson & Sons,

1964). Cf. also his *Theologie des Neuen Testaments,* Vol. 1 (Göttingen: Vandenhoeck & Ruprecht, 1975).

8. For a helpful discussion of Easter language, cf. X. Léon-Dufour, *Resurrection and the Message of Easter* (London: G. Chapman, 1971).

9. Although the RSV places Lk. 24:12 (Peter's visit to the tomb) in the margin, there is good textual reason for including this in the text of Luke's chapter. In John 20, Peter and the beloved disciple go to the tomb.

10. Hans von Campenhausen, "The Events of Easter and the Empty Tomb," in *Tradition and Life in the Church* (Fortress Press, 1968) has sought to reconstruct the order of the Easter events. Karl Barth, *Church Dogmatics* IV/1 (Edinburgh: T. & T. Clark, 1956), p. 149, calls this 1952 essay a "remarkable investigation" but one that does not help us.

11. Cf. C. H. Dodd, *According to the Scriptures* (Charles Scribner's Sons, 1953); also B. Lindars, *New Testament Apologetic* (Philadelphia: Westminster Press, 1961; London: SCM Press 1961).

12. Klaus Berger, *Die Auferstehung des Propheten und die Erhöhung des Menschensohnes. Traditionsgeschichtliche Untersuchungen zur Deutung des Geschickes Jesu in frühchristlichen Texten* (Göttingen: Vandenhoeck & Ruprecht, 1976).

13. Peter Stuhlmacher, "Das Bekenntnis zur Auferstehung Jesu von den Toten und die biblische Theologie," *Zeitschrift für Theologie und Kirche,* Dec. 1973. Cf. also his *Schriftauslegung auf dem Wege zur biblischen Theologie* (Göttingen: Vandenhoeck & Ruprecht, 1975) in which he says that a biblical theology of the New Testament "can and must be open toward the Old Testament as the decisive foundation of the formulation of the tradition of the New Testament" (p. 127), as quoted in Gerhard Hasel, *New Testament Theology: Basic Issues in the Current Debate* (Wm. B. Eerdmans, 1978), p. 172. In this he parallels the appeal to canonical exegesis made by Brevard Childs, *Biblical Theology in Crisis* (Westminster Press, 1970), and by J. A. Sanders, *Torah and Canon* (Fortress Press, 1972).

14. The song of Hannah is frequently cited in this connection. Cf. Stuhlmacher, "Das Bekenntnis," p. 388; Léon-Dufour, *Resurrection and the Message of Easter,* p. 18, etc.

15. The most persuasive appeal to this text is in Lindars, *New Testament Apologetic,* pp. 64–66. Cf. also H. K. McArthur, "On the

Third Day," *New Testament Studies,* Oct. 1971, who cites rabbinic evidence that Hos. 6:2 was regularly associated with the resurrection of the dead (giving eleven examples). While the rabbinic evidence is late, R. H. Fuller, *The Formation of the Resurrection Narratives* (Macmillan Co., 1971), thinks it quite probable "that we have here a long-standing apocalyptic explanation not otherwise attested," and concludes that it would be "the natural one to look for, since apocalyptic was the matrix of the earliest Christian kerygma and colors every part of these primitive formulae" (p. 26).

16. While we shall deal with this more fully in a discussion of "the third day" in Chapter II, it is appropriate here to mention "A Suggestion Concerning the Meaning of 1 Cor. 15:4," by Bruce M. Metzger, *Journal of Theological Studies,* 1957. He proposed that we give up looking for a "third day" altogether in terms of the Old Testament Scriptures, suggesting that the clauses "on the third day" and "according to the scriptures" in 1 Corinthians 15 are coordinate clauses, both modifying "that he was raised." He finds an analogous use of such coordinate clauses in 1 Macc. 7:16, where "in one day" and "in accordance with the word" appear: "So they trusted him [Alcimus]; but he seized sixty of them and killed them in one day, in accordance with the word which was written,

" 'The flesh of the saints and their blood
they poured out round about Jerusalem,
and there was none to bury them.' " (1 Macc. 7:16–17)

Here, certainly, the quotation from Ps. 79:3 contains no mention of time. However, Metzger's argument from 1 Maccabees illustrates only the possibility of style rather than actually demonstrating that the verse in 1 Corinthians 15 is to be taken in parallel structure. Cf. E. L. Bode, *The First Easter Morning: The Gospel Accounts of the Women's Visit to the Tomb of Jesus* (Rome: Biblical Institute Press, 1970), p. 117. Bode holds, as do most scholars, that "the order of the present wording seems to indicate that the scripture reference is to the third day." He is not content to confine this to Hos. 6:2.

17. For a documented review of the "History-of-Religion Background and the Analogy Question," cf. Alsup, *Post-Resurrection Appearance Stories,* pp. 214ff. In the mystery religions, the dying and rising of cult deities often have a close association with the annual cycle of the seasons. In the Hellenistic world we also have stories of particular individuals ("divine men") who were singled

out for their virtue, wisdom, and power. Such persons sometimes appear to others after death. Romulus is the legendary founder of Rome. Apollonius of Tyana was a wandering teacher and miracle worker of the first century.

18. On the literary relationship between theophany and resurrection appearances, cf. Léon-Dufour, *Resurrection and the Message of Easter,* pp. 34, 160, 214; A. R. C. Leaney, "Theophany, Resurrection, and History," in *Studia Evangelica,* Vol. 5, ed. F. L. Cross (Berlin: Akademie Verlag, 1968); Goppelt, *Theologie,* Vol. 1, p. 291; especially Alsup, *Post-Resurrection Appearance Stories,* pp. 214–239, with examination of the relevant texts.

19. Other characteristic theophany stories are found in Judges 13 and 1 Samuel 3. In the Apocrypha, cf. Tobit 5 and 12.

20. Cf. Samuel Terrien, *The Elusive Presence: Toward a New Biblical Theology* (Harper & Row, 1978), pp. 428–440. He holds that "the literary type of the prophetic vision, with its call and commission, has been inserted into the patriarchal-legend pattern of epiphanic visitation" and "has been transformed into a new literary type" (pp. 429f.).

21. Cf. J. A. Wharton, "The Occasion of the Word of God: An Unguarded Essay on the Character of the Old Testament as the Memory of God's Story with Israel," *Austin Seminary Bulletin,* Faculty Edition, Sept. 1968. Cf. D. Ritschl and H. O. Jones, *"Story" als Rohmaterial der Theologie* (Munich: Chr. Kaiser Verlag, 1976), for a development of this concept with particular reference to Wharton's article. Cf. also H. Frei, *The Eclipse of Biblical Narrative* (Yale University Press, 1974). For a different way of combating "historicism" as this has often been applied to the Bible and especially to the resurrection of Jesus, cf. Alan Richardson, *History Sacred and Profane* (Westminster Press, 1964).

22. O'Collins, *What Are They Saying About the Resurrection?* pp. 46f.

23. Léon-Dufour, *Resurrection and the Message of Easter,* p. xvi.

24. Especially Willi Marxsen, "The Resurrection of Jesus as a Historical Problem," in *Significance of the Message of the Resurrection,* ed. Moule. Marxsen has developed his views in *The Resurrection of Jesus of Nazareth* (Philadelphia: Fortress Press, 1970; London: SCM Press, 1970). Taking his cue from Marxsen, Peter C. Hodgson has written a provocative volume entitled *Jesus—Word*

and Presence (Fortress Press, 1971) in which he says: "I propose to dispense with this salvation-history schema and its neat chronological distinctions—distinctions that rupture the unity of temporal-historical experience, reduce the resurrection to the level of a miraculous fact, and elevate the present dominion of Christ to an other-worldly realm" (p. 222). He proposes to understand the resurrection in its most comprehensive sense possible "as an event embracing all three modes of time but with a peculiar focus upon the present." Appealing to Paul's use of the perfect tense in 1 Corinthians 15, he holds that "the argument moves from the present through the past into the future and embraces the modes of time in a dynamic unity." Like Marxsen, he views the present as the fulcrum from which inferences are drawn about the past and the future.

25. Of the many studies on this formula, cf. Hans Conzelmann, "On the Analysis of the Confessional Formula in 1 Corinthians 15:3–5," *Interpretation,* Jan. 1966.

26. Cf. G. Kegel, *Auferstehung Jesu—Auferstehung der Toten* (Gütersloher Verlagshaus Gerd Mohn, 1970). If it strikes us as strange that the text does not speak of the resurrection of Jesus but of the general resurrection of the dead, the explanation can only be that the resurrection of the dead was seen as already actualized and begun in the person of Jesus (p. 32). O. Michel, *Der Brief an die Römer* (Göttingen: Vandenhoeck & Ruprecht, 1957), interprets the formula in similar fashion: with the resurrection of Jesus the resurrection of the dead has begun. W. Kramer, *Christ, Lord, Son of God* (London: SCM Press, 1966), Studies in Biblical Theology, 1st series, No. 50, p. 110, recognizes that *ex anastaseōs nekrōn* is ambiguous and that *ek nekrōn* would make clearer that the resurrection of Jesus is intended, but he believes that the sense demands a translation such as is provided in the RSV: "his resurrection from the dead." H. Schlier, "Zu Rom 1,3f," in *Neues Testament und Geschichte,* ed. H. Baltensweiler and B. Reicke (Tübingen: J. C. B. Mohr [Paul Siebeck], 1972), does not deal with this phrase of the formula but is more concerned with the history of the formula itself, finding three stages in its development.

27. Cf. Ernst Käsemann, "The Beginnings of Christian Theology," in *New Testament Questions of Today* (Fortress Press, 1969).

28. To the question: "What are the manifold benefits that come to us from his resurrection?" the catechism replies: "Three. By it

righteousness is obtained for us (Rom. 4:24); it is a sure pledge of our future immortality (1 Cor. 15); and even now by its virtue we are raised to newness of life, that we may obey God's will by pure and holy living." The translation is by Gabriel Vahanian, in Karl Barth, *The Faith of the Church: A Commentary on the Apostles' Creed According to Calvin's Catechism* (Meridian Books, 1958), p. 101. The French and Latin texts of this catechism are in *Calvini Opera* VI (*Corpus Reformatorum* XXXIV). However, in the 1559 edition of the *Institutes* (II. xvi.13), the order is reversed, so that the present precedes the future benefits.

Chapter II. The Resurrection as Past Event

1. John Knox, *Christ the Lord* (1945), in *Jesus: Lord and Christ* (Harper & Brothers, 1958), p. 120.

2. For the text of this noncanonical document, with an introduction by Chr. Maurer, cf. Edgar Hennecke, *New Testament Apocrypha*, ed. Wilhelm Schneemelcher, trans. R. McL. Wilson, Vol. 1 (Philadelphia: Westminster Press, 1963; London: Lutterworth Press, 1963), pp. 179–187. The description of the resurrection reads: "When now those soldiers saw this, they awakened the centurion and the elders—for they also were there to assist at the watch. And whilst they were relating what they had seen, they saw again three men come out from the sepulcre, and two of them sustaining the other, and a cross following them, and the heads of the two reaching to heaven, but that of him who was led of them by the hand overpassing the heavens. And they heard a voice out of the heavens crying, 'Hast thou preached to them that sleep?', and from the cross there was heard the answer, 'Yea.' " (p. 186)

3. Cf. J. McLeman, *Resurrection Then and Now* (London: Hodder & Stoughton, 1965), Ch. 16, "Event or Conviction?" He concludes: "The conclusion therefore that this phenomenon at the centre of the post-crucifixion experience of the disciples is a conviction rather than an event is continuous with what we have found in our survey of the history of the resurrection idea. Historical necessity wove the garment. The Christian conviction survived, but in a grosser form and at the expense of the pure leap of faith which is its source and origin" (p. 169).

4. Rudolf Bultmann, "The Primitive Christian Kerygma and the Historical Jesus," in *The Historical Jesus and the Kerygmatic Christ,*

trans. and ed. Carl E. Braaten and R. A. Harrisville (Abingdon Press, 1964), p. 42.

5. Karl Barth, "Biblical Questions, Insights, and Vistas" (1920), in *The Word of God and the Word of Man* (Pilgrim Press, 1928), p. 90. This is cited by Van A. Harvey, *The Historian and the Believer* (Macmillan Co., 1966), p. 154, but without the last clause.

6. Karl Barth, *The Epistle to the Romans* (1921), 6th ed. (Oxford University Press, 1933), p. 30.

7. Karl Barth, *Church Dogmatics* III/2 (Edinburgh: T. & T. Clark, 1960), pp. 442f.

8. This change is noted by Harvey, *The Historian and the Believer,* and by R. C. Crawford, "The Resurrection of Christ," in *Theology,* April 1972.

9. Cf. T. F. Torrance, *Space, Time and Incarnation* (Oxford University Press, 1969), p. 90: "Hence it is quite impossible for Christian theology to be indifferent to questions of historical facticity, for any construct of Christ that has no rooting in actual history can only be a vehicle of our fantasies. Thus, for example, the doctrine of the resurrection cannot do without its empirical correlate in the empty tomb; cut that away and it becomes nonsensical." His treatment of Easter faith receives fuller treatment in *Space, Time and Resurrection* (Grand Rapids: Wm. B. Eerdmans Publishing Co., 1977; Edinburgh: Handsel Press, 1976). Further references to Torrance will be to this second volume.

10. Hodgson, note 24 to Chapter 1.

11. Cf. D. Fascher, "Anastasis-Resurrectio-Auferstehung," in *Zeitschrift für die neutestamentliche Wissenschaft und die Kunde der älteren Kirche,* 1941.

12. Léon-Dufour, *Resurrection and the Message of Easter,* p. 14, thinks it highly probable that New Testament tradition progressively attributes to Christ what was first described as the work of God.

13. Cf. Torrance, *Space, Time and Resurrection,* Ch. 3.

14. Quoted in A. M. Ramsey, *The Resurrection of Christ* (Westminster Press, 1946), p. 9.

15. Cf. W. Michaelis, *Die Erscheinungen des Auferstandenen* (Basel: Verlag von Heinrich Majer, 1944), pp. 108f. Cf. his article on *horaō* in Kittel-Friedrich, *Theological Dictionary of the New Testament,* Vol. 5 (Wm. B. Eerdmans, 1967), pp. 355ff.

16. Cf. G. Delling on *hēmera* in Kittel-Friedrich, Vol. 2, p. 950; also article on *treis* in *ibid.,* Vol. 8.

17. Cf. Bode, *The First Easter Morning,* Ch. 7. His citation of the data regarding Gen. 22:4 is found on pp. 119f.:

> "Commenting on the verse, the midrash Genesis Rabba states that God never leaves the just man in distress longer than three days. This midrash refers to seven texts to illustrate God's salvation on the third day:
>
>> It is written, 'After two days he will revive us, on the third day he will raise us up that we may live in his presence' (Hos 6:2). For example, on the third day of the tribal ancestors: 'And Joseph said unto them the third day: 'This do and live' (Gn 42:18); on the third day of revelation: 'And it came to pass on the third day, when it was morning' (Ex 19:16); on the third day of the spies: 'And hide yourselves there three days' (Jos 2:16); on the third day of Jonah: 'And Jonah was in the belly of the fish three days and three nights' (Jon 2:1); on the third day of those returning from the exile: 'And we abode there three days' (Ezr 8:32); on the third day of the resurrection: 'After two days he will revive us, on the third day he will raise us up'; on the third day of Esther: 'Now it came to pass on the third day that Esther put on her royal apparel' (Est 5:1), that is, she put on the royal apparel of her ancestor. For whose sake? The rabbis say: For the sake of the third day, when revelation took place. Rabbi Levi maintained: In the merit of what Abraham did on the third day, as it says.
>
> "Thus is emphasized that the third day is the day of salvation, of rescue from great need and threatening danger and of certain hope in divine assistance."

Bode recognizes that it is difficult to date the material contained in midrash and targum. Genesis Rabba is probably from the fourth to the sixth century A.D. But "it would seem strange to us that such an explicit development of the third-day-salvation then would have developed only after the Christian preaching of Jesus' resurrection on the third day. Such a post-Christian emphasis would only add to the strength of the Christian cause" (p. 123).

Another attempt to so account for the "third day" motif can be found in C. Mackay, "The Third Day," in *Church Quarterly Review,* 1963, but Bode is methodologically more convincing.

18. Bode, *The First Easter Morning,* p. 125.

19. Von Campenhausen, *Tradition and Life in the Church,* p. 46. Long before von Campenhausen, Kirsopp Lake, *The Historical Evidence for the Resurrection of Jesus Christ* (G. P. Putnam's Sons, 1907), p. 254, had said substantially the same: "It is impossible that the use of the Old Testament prophecy by itself led to the choice of the third day. . . . Thus it is so probable as almost to be certain that the choice of the third day was bound up in the early church from the beginning with the experience of the women."

20. Cf. Willy Rordorf, *Sunday* (Philadelphia: Westminster Press, 1968; London: SCM Press, 1968), p. 219. Rordorf traces the origin of the Christian Sunday to an evening appearance of Jesus at Easter; Bode, *The First Easter Morning,* traces it to the finding of the empty tomb on Easter morning.

21. C. H. Giblin, "Structural and Thematic Correlations in the Burial-Resurrection Narrative," in *New Testament Studies,* April 1975.

22. So Bode, *The First Easter Morning,* p. 126.

23. Cf. Knox, *Jesus Lord and Christ,* pp. 121f.: "Like the good dramatist he was, he [Mark] only points to them [the appearances], preferring to end his book with the marvelously impressive fact which had only recently made its way into the tradition, or, if earlier, had not been widely known."

24. Maurice Goguel, *La Foi à la résurrection de Jesus dans le christianisme primitif* (Paris: Librairie Ernest Laroux, 1933), p. 445.

25. Cf. G. W. H. Lampe and D. M. MacKinnon, *The Resurrection: A Dialogue,* ed. William Purcell (Philadelphia: Westminster Press, 1967; London: A. R. Mowbray & Co., 1966), pp. 57–58. Lampe suggested that to understand the resurrection as bodily and to add the empty grave was greatly stimulated by early Christian reflection on Ps. 16:10: "When Christians searched the Old Testament for texts bearing on the Resurrection they would be struck by Psalm 16:10. . . . This prophecy was a powerful weapon in the armoury of Christian apologetic. It is cited in Acts 2:27 and Acts 13:35. It would immediately suggest that the raising of Jesus ought to be conceived in terms of a physical resurrection of the body. From that point the story would inevitably come to be built up, as we can see it growing in the Gospels." Lampe considers the speeches

in Acts as reliable evidence for the way in which Luke, and the church for which he wrote, understood the gospel, but not for the original preaching of Peter and the other apostles.

26. Hans Werner Bartsch, "Der Ursprung des Osterglaubens," *Theologische Zeitschrift*, 1974, p. 18, suggested that in the conclusion to the passion narrative's account of the burial of Jesus one can still detect the residue of an early apocalyptic coloring that shatters our world of time and space, holding that Matthew's tradition had the apocalyptic Son of Man (under the guise of "the angel of the Lord") roll the stone away. But, Bartsch contends, Matthew displaced this end time vision of heavenly radiance with the legend of the empty grave.

27. For other studies on the place of Ps. 16:10 in the New Testament message of the resurrection, cf. Lindars, *New Testament Apologetic*, pp. 38–45 (who sees it as pre-apologetic); Ian H. Marshall, "The Resurrection in the Acts of the Apostles," in *Apostolic History and the Gospel*, ed. Ward Gasque and Ralph Martin (Grand Rapids: Wm. B. Eerdmans, 1970; Exeter, Devon: Paternoster Press, 1970), who questions the claim of later apologetic appropriation by Ulrich Wilckens, *Die Missionsreden der Apostelgeschichte* (Neukirchen-Vluyn: Neukirchener Verlag, 1963).

28. So L. Schenke, *Auferstehungsverkündigung und leeres Grab* (Stuttgart: Verlag Katholisches Bibelwerk, 1968). This has found favor in many Roman Catholic scholars—e.g., J. Delorme, "The Resurrection and Jesus' Tomb," Ch. 4 in *The Resurrection and Modern Biblical Thought*, by P. de Surgy et al. (Corpus Books, 1970). Bode, *The First Easter Morning*, p. 131, concludes that this hypothesis lacks evidence.

29. This argument has less weight if one follows the dating proposed by J. A. T. Robinson, *Redating the New Testament* (Philadelphia: Westminster Press, 1976; London: SCM Press, 1976). Robinson dates all the New Testament documents prior to A.D. 70 and suggests that Mark himself was "certainly back in Jerusalem" in 46 or 47, even though his Gospel may reflect the Neronian persecution.

30. Ulrich Wilckens, *Resurrection, Biblical Testimony to the Resurrection: An Historical Examination and Explanation* (Atlanta: John Knox Press, 1978; Edinburgh: Saint Andrew Press, 1977).

31. Cf. such critiques as in Schenke and in Alsup. The grave story lacks Old Testament references and allusions which mark the passion story. Alsup, *Post-Resurrection Appearance Stories*, p. 91, com-

ments that this is "a thorny problem for Wilckens' thesis." Other criticisms, such as the repetition of the women's names, are enumerated in Schenke, *Auferstehungsverkündigung und leeres Grab.*

32. For example, in the Lord's appearance to the women in Matthew, his words only repeat the angelic message. In Jn. 20: 11–18, on the other hand, we have a characteristic appearance story in which features such as the lack of recognition are present. But the literary "seams" are evident because the references to Mary (vs. 1, 11–18) are interrupted by the story of Peter and the beloved disciple.

33. In *Face to Face with the Turin Shroud,* ed. Peter Jennings (London: A. R. Mowbray & Co., 1978), J. A. T. Robinson compares the Gospel accounts of the burial with the shroud's indication of burial customs. Without assuming any conclusions as to the shroud's antiquity or authenticity, he writes: "The first thing that the genuineness of the Shroud would shake is the theory that the whole story of the empty tomb is an invention of the early church" (p. 77).

34. The first to subject the question of locality to full investigation was E. Lohmeyer, *Galiläa und Jerusalem* (Göttingen: Vandenhoeck & Ruprecht, 1936).

35. Cf. C. F. D. Moule, "From Defendant to Judge—and Deliverer: An Inquiry Into the Use and Limitations of the Theme of Vindication in the New Testament," in his *The Phenomenon of the New Testament,* Studies in Biblical Theology, 2d series, No. 1 (London: SCM Press, 1967).

36. The RSV New Testament uses the verb "to vindicate" five times for three Greek verbs. See Clinton Morrison, *An Analytical Concordance to the Revised Standard Version of the New Testament* (Westminster Press, 1979). The RSV Old Testament uses "to vindicate" fifteen times and the noun fourteen times. Cf. J. W. Ellison, *Nelson's Complete Concordance of the Revised Standard Version Bible* (Thomas Nelson & Sons, 1957). The latter is not an analytical concordance and does not show the Hebrew words so rendered.

37. Moule, *Phenomenon,* p. 98.

38. On the Roman Catholic side, cf. such works as Francis X. Durrwell, *The Resurrection* (Sheed & Ward, 1960), and D. M. Stanley, *Christ's Resurrection in Pauline Soteriology* (Rome: Pontifical Biblical Institute, 1961). On the Protestant side, cf. Markus Barth and V. Fletcher, *Acquittal by Resurrection* (Holt, Rinehart &

Winston, 1964), and Markus Barth, *Justification* (Wm. B. Eerdmans, 1971). A further reminder that Western theology needs to recover the emphasis of the Eastern Church on the resurrection as redemption is made by Dietrich Ritschl, *Memory and Hope: An Inquiry Concerning the Presence of Christ* (Macmillan Co., 1967).

39. Torrance, *Space, Time and Resurrection,* p. 62.

40. The opposite view is expressed by G. W. H. Lampe, *God as Spirit* (Oxford: Clarendon Press, 1977), pp. 156f.: "It is sometimes said that by an act of raising Jesus from the dead God 'gave him to be visible' to his friends who had deserted or denied him, so that through him fellowship between God and man might be restored. The resurrection of Jesus and his appearances to his disciples would thus be seen as a means of reconciliation and forgiveness. It does not seem, however, that the Easter stories in the New Testament do in fact convey this meaning. On the contrary, although the disciples are said in the Lucan and Johannine stories to have rejoiced at the Lord's presence, these narratives do not suggest a resumption of Jesus' relations with his followers at the point where they had been broken off by his arrest. It is specially remarkable that in the canonical Gospels there is no account whatever of a reconciliation, of penitence on the part of disciples, and of forgiveness by Jesus, such as one would expect if the Easter stories were actual history rather than mythical pictures of the continuing communion of believers with Christ and of the inspiration that launched the Church's mission.

"There is not even any explicit mention of a restoration of Peter to fellowship with the Lord whom he had denied, although the tradition that Peter experienced the first of the resurrection appearances is very early. At most, a reversal and cancellation of his denial of Jesus may be implied in the appendix to the Fourth Gospel. . . .

"Not only does there seem to have been no need for the restoration to fellowship with God of those who had rejected Jesus to have been effected through a resurrection-event, a personal return of Jesus in visible form, but in fact there were no appearances at all to those who had positively rejected and condemned him." (Used by permission of Oxford University Press.)

41. Cf. Ian H. Marshall, *Luke: Historian and Theologian* (Grand Rapids: Zondervan Publishing House, 1971; London: Paternoster

Press 1970), and especially his article, "The Resurrection in the Acts of the Apostles," cited in note 27 above.

42. Torrance, *Space, Time and Resurrection,* p. 63.

43. M. Barth, *Justification,* p. 54.

44. Quoted in H. R. Niebuhr, *The Meaning of Revelation* (Macmillan Co., 1941), p. 191.

45. Ritschl, *Memory and Hope,* p. 215.

46. Albert Camus, *The Myth of Sisyphus and Other Essays* (Random House, Vintage Books, 1959), p. 90.

47. Gerhard Gloege, *The Day of His Coming* (Fortress Press, 1963). Cf. his epilogue, "The Rescue of Sisyphus," p. 293.

48. Cf. Bo Reicke, *The Disobedient Spirits and Christian Baptism: A Study of I Pet. iii.19 and Its Context* (Copenhagen: E. Munksgaard, 1946).

49. I use the wording of this hymn as found in *The Hymnbook* (Philadelphia, 1955).

50. George Herbert, *The Temple & A Priest to the Temple* (E. P. Dutton, n.d.), "Sunday," p. 73. Herbert's dates are 1593–1633.

51. Wilckens, *Resurrection,* pp. 13–15.

52. *Ibid.,* p. 15. Wilckens maintains that the "more than 500" who had come together in order to form a community of disciples were now themselves "all collectively validated, by an appearance of his, as God's community for salvation at the Day of Judgment. These community members of the beginning then held a prominent specially-singled-out position of honour within the Jerusalem primitive community—so Paul can assume that they were all individually known." Others have sought to link the 500 with Pentecost. No attempt at identification has been persuasive.

53. Fuller, *The Formation of the Resurrection Narratives,* p. 23.

54. Cf. Walther Schmithals, *The Office of Apostle in the Early Church* (Abingdon Press, 1969). But cf. Rengstorf's article in Kittel-Friedrich, Vol. 1, and also his *Apostolate and Ministry* (Concordia Publishing House, 1969). For a shorter article, cf. M. H. Shepherd, Jr., in *The Interpreter's Dictionary of the Bible,* Vol. 1 (Abingdon Press, 1962).

55. Fuller, *The Formation of the Resurrection Narratives,* p. 45.

56. Cf. E. Sjöberg, in Kittel-Friedrich, Vol. 6, p. 385.

57. Cf. Hendrikus Berkhof, *Christ, the Meaning of History* (John Knox Press, 1966), p. 63; also his *Well-Founded Hope* (John Knox

Press, 1969), pp. 23f. Cf. also my *Biblical Images* (Hawthorn Books, 1974), Ch. 4.

58. Our concern here is the final canonical shape of the gospel, not with the stages of its redaction. For the latter, we may consult the commentaries.

Appendix to Chapter II

1. With slight revision this appendix reprints my article first published in *A.D.* March 1974, and published as chapter 3 in *Biblical Images*. It represents a development of suggestions made in Wilckens, *Resurrection,* p. 41.

2. Wilckens associates Ps. 55:12f. with Peter's denial, but cf. Bertil Gärtner, *Iscariot* (Fortress Press, 1971), Ch. 5, "Judas Typology in the New Testament: Ahithophel as a Type." He points out that the targum of Ps. 55 reads Ahithophel's name into the psalm text. Rabbinic tradition linked the suicide of Ahithophel with Ps. 55:23.

3. G. C. Morgan, *The Crises of the Christ* (Fleming H. Revell, 1903), p. 301.

Chapter III. The Resurrection as Disclosure of the Future

1. Torrance, *Space, Time and Resurrection,* p. 145.

2. Paul Minear, *Christian Hope and the Second Coming* (Westminster Press, 1954), Ch. 1. Cf. also C. F. D. Moule, *The Meaning of Hope* (Philadelphia: Fortress Press, 1963; London: Highway Press, 1953).

3. This point is also made by Ritschl, *Memory and Hope,* p. 13: "Theology, i.e., the reflection upon these dimensions in the light of the present situation, is obliged to extend and constantly renew the invitation to 'hope backward' into the realm of memory and to 'remember forward' into the realm of hope. . . . Hope provides not only a 'mood' but the matrix of future events; it 'creates the reality of tomorrow.' "

4. Jacques Ellul, *Apocalypse* (Seabury Press, 1977), esp. p. 49.

5. *Ibid.,* pp. 109f. on Rev. 19:13. After considering other interpretations, he says: "The robe dipped in blood is not different from the white robe of the first vision: it is not red with the blood of enemies; it is white by the purification obtained through the cross.

This Word, personified in the horseman, is then victorious: the sole victory of God is the fact of his Word (the Word incarnate, crucified, and nevertheless also and at the same time, the same as the Creator Word of the first day). He wins no other victory. He has no other weapon." This is also the interpretation of George E. Ladd, *A Commentary on the Revelation of John* (Wm. B. Eerdmans, 1972).

6. As cited in A. F. J. Klijn, *An Introduction to the New Testament* (Leiden: E. J. Brill, 1969), p. 220.

7. Cf. Massey H. Shepherd, Jr., *The Paschal Liturgy and the Apocalypse* (John Knox Press, 1960). This is overdrawn, but cf. L. Mowry, "Revelation 4–5 and Early Christian Liturgical Usage," in *Journal of Biblical Literature*, March 1952.

8. Cf. C. H. Dodd, "The Appearances of the Risen Christ: An Essay in Form-Criticism of the Gospels," in *Studies in the Gospels: Essays in Memory of R. H. Lightfoot,* ed. D. E. Nineham (Oxford: Blackwell, 1955). Cf. also Alsup, *Post-Resurrection Appearance Stories,* pp. 141ff.

9. Cf. J. A. T. Robinson, *Jesus and His Coming* (Philadelphia: Westminster Press, 1979; London: SCM, 1957), p. 45, for the view that Jesus himself understood the "clouds of heaven" as "going up" (as in Dan. 7), to express his confidence in speedy vindication.

10. C. F. D. Moule, *Origin of Christology* (Cambridge University Press, 1977), p. 53.

11. J. A. T. Robinson, *The Body* (Chicago: Henry Regnery, 1952; Philadelphia: Westminster Press, 1977), p. 49.

12. Cf. J. A. T. Robinson, "Resurrection in the NT," in *The Interpreter's Dictionary of the Bible,* Vol. 4. Cf. also Robinson's article, "The Shroud and the New Testament," in *Face to Face with the Turin Shroud* ed. Jennings; cf. J. A. T. Robinson, *The Human Face of God* (Philadelphia: Westminster Press, 1973; London: SCM, 1973), Ch. 4.

13. Robinson, *The Human Face of God,* pp. 140f. The italic is his.

14. In John H. Leith, *Creeds of the Churches* (Doubleday & Co., Anchor Books, 1963), p. 267. Italics mine.

15. *Ibid.,* p. 204. Italics mine.

16. Robinson, *The Body,* p. 51.

17. Cf. my article, "I Cor. 15:24–28 and the Future of Jesus Christ," in a forthcoming Festschrift in memory of Stuart D. Currie, *Texts and Testaments,* ed. W. E. March, to be published by

Trinity University Press in 1980. The article examines Marcellus, Calvin, and A. A. van Ruler. Marcellus' view is treated also in Aloys Grillmeier, *Christ in Christian Tradition,* vol. 1, 2d rev. ed.; 3 vols., vol. 1 (John Knox Press, 1975), and in E. Schendel, *Herrschaft und Unterwerfung Christi* (Tübingen: J. C. B. Mohr [Paul Siebeck], 1971).

18. Cf. Adriaan Geense, *Auferstehung und Offenbarung* (Göttingen: Vandenhoeck & Ruprecht, 1971), Ch. 6.

19. Jules Isaac, *Jesus and Israel* (Holt, Rinehart & Winston, 1971), p. 358.

20. D. R. A. Hare, *The Theme of Jewish Persecution of Christians in the Gospel According to Matthew* (Cambridge University Press, 1967), Ch. 5.

21. *Ibid.,* p. 170.

22. Cf. the Bristol paper of the World Council of Churches, "The Church and the Jewish People" (Geneva: WCC Faith and Order paper 50, 1968). Cf. H. Berkhof, "Israel as a Theological Problem in the Christian Church," in *Journal of Ecumenical Studies,* Vol. 6, 1969. Cf. also Markus Barth, *Israel and the Church* (John Knox Press, 1969).

23. A statement on "The Hope of Israel" was signed by twenty-four delegates at the Evanston Assembly. Cf. D. P. Gaines, *The World Council of Churches: A Study of Its Background and History* (Peterborough, N.H., 1966), pp. 488f.

24. From "A Declaration of Faith," submitted to the 116th General Assembly of the Presbyterian Church in the U.S. (Atlanta: Materials Distribution Service, 341 Ponce de Leon Ave., N.E., 1976).

25. So Hans J. Margull, *Hope in Action* (Muhlenberg Press, 1962).

26. Kegel, *Auferstehung Jesu—Auferstehung der Toten,* p. 45.

27. As cited in H. C. C. Cavallin, *Life After Death: An Enquiry Into the Jewish Background* (Lund: CWK Gleerup, 1974), p. 177.

28. *Ibid.,* p. 200.

29. C. F. D. Moule, "St. Paul and Dualism: The Pauline Conception of the Resurrection," in *New Testament Studies,* Jan. 1966, p. 107. Robinson, *The Human Face of God,* p. 140, is "doubtful of this exegesis, attractive as it is."

30. Moule, "St. Paul and Dualism."

31. E.g., J. A. Schep, *The Nature of the Resurrection Body* (Wm. B. Eerdmans, 1964).

32. Cf. Robinson, *The Body*, p. 81. To separate 1 Corinthians 15 from the rest of Paul's writing has also led "to the supposition that Paul thought of the resurrection of the body in a purely individualistic manner. But this is quite untrue even of I Cor. 15. It is instructive to notice how he refuses to answer the question in the individual form in which his imaginary objector raises it."

33. Jürgen Moltmann, *Theology of Hope* (New York: Harper & Row, 1967; London: SCM, 1967), p. 32. He also points to Dante's words.

34. *Ibid.*, p. 17.

35. *Ibid.*, p. 20. It is interesting to compare Moltmann's sequence with that suggested in our approach. His *Theology of Hope* was followed by *The Crucified God* (New York: Harper & Row, 1974; London: SCM, 1974) and by *The Church in the Power of the Spirit* (New York: Harper & Row, 1977; London: SCM, 1977). In his preface (pp. xvi–xvii) of the last named, he comments on the trilogy: "Consequently the books dovetail into one another and their subject-matter overlaps. It is true, however, that I was impelled theologically from the one book to the other and had to shift my perspectives, the better to understand the wealth of God's dealings with the world. That is why I shifted the emphasis from 'the resurrection of the crucified Jesus' in *Theology of Hope* to 'the cross of the risen Christ' in *The Crucified God*. Both perspectives would be incomplete if 'the sending of the Spirit' . . . were not added."

Chapter IV. The Significance of the Resurrection for the Present

1. Cf. P. H. Williams, Jr., "The Future Tense of God Is Yahweh: A Study of Isaiah 40–55," in *Austin Seminary Bulletin*, Faculty Edition, April 1969.

2. E.g., Claus Westermann, *Isaiah 40–66: A Commentary*, The Old Testament Library (Philadelphia: Westminster Press, 1969; London: SCM Press, 1969), p. 212.

3. In Rom. 8:23 Paul speaks of "waiting" for the adoption as sons, while in 8:15 "you have received" the spirit of sonship. Both verses use the word *huiothesia*.

4. E. Best, *One Body in Christ* (London: SPCK, 1955), p. 45.

5. Contra Rudolf Bultmann, *The Gospel of John: A Commentary*

(Philadelphia: Westminster Press, 1971; Oxford: Basil Blackwell, 1971), p. 696: "The doubt of Thomas is representative of the common attitude of men, who cannot believe without seeing miracles (4.48). As the miracle is a concession to the weakness of man, so is the appearance of the Risen Jesus a concession to the weakness of the disciples. Fundamentally they ought not to need it!"

6. Raymond E. Brown, *The Gospel According to John*, Vol. 2 (Doubleday & Co., 1970), p. 1049.

7. Hendrikus Berkhof, *The Doctrine of the Holy Spirit* (John Knox Press, 1964), p. 15.

8. *Ibid.*, p. 19.

9. J. D. G. Dunn, "I Corinthians 15:45—'Last Adam, Lifegiving Spirit,' " in *Christ and Spirit*, ed. B. Lindars and S. Smalley (Cambridge University Press, 1973), p. 127.

10. Cf. I. Herrmann, *Kyrios und Pneuma* (Munich: Kösel Verlag, 1961). He is frequently cited, e.g., by Berkhof, *Doctrine of the Holy Spirit*, p. 25.

11. J. D. G. Dunn, "II Corinthians III, 17—'The Lord is the Spirit,' " *Journal of Theological Studies*, Oct. 1970; C. F. D. Moule, *'kathaper apo kyriou pneumatos,'* in *Neues Testament und Geschichte*, ed. Baltensweiler and Reicke. This interpretation is also suggested by G. Hendry, *The Holy Spirit in Christian Theology* (Philadelphia: Westminster Press, 1956; London: SCM, 1957), p. 24, but without the exegetical detail offered by Dunn and Moule.

12. Berkhof, *Doctrine of the Holy Spirit*, p. 28.

13. Berkhof raises this question and begins with the mission. Cf. his second chapter.

14. Selby, *Look for the Living*, p. 135.

15. For a discussion of Jn. 20:23, cf. Brown, *The Gospel According to John*, Vol. 2, pp. 1039ff.

16. Hendry, *The Holy Spirit in Christian Theology*, pp. 23f.

17. W. C. van Unnik, "Jesus: Anathema or Kyrios (1 Cor. 12:3)," in *Christ and Spirit in the New Testament*, p. 124.

18. *Ibid.*

19. E.g., A. Come, *Human Spirit and Holy Spirit* (Westminster Press, 1959); Hendry, *The Holy Spirit in Christian Theology;* Berkhof, *Doctrine of the Holy Spirit.* Cf. also Berkhof, *Christelijk Geloof* (Nijkerk: G. F. Callenbach, 1973). For more extended discussion, cf. K. Barth, *Church Dogmatics* I/1 as over against Leonard Hodgson, *The Doctrine of the Spirit* (Charles Scribner's Sons, 1944).

20. Berkhof, *Doctrine of the Holy Spirit,* pp. 118f.

21. *Ibid.*

22. Lampe, *God as Spirit,* p. 157.

23. *Ibid.,* p. 158. Lampe closes his book with a summary of his own view: "I believe in the Divinity of our Lord and Saviour Jesus Christ, in the sense that the one God, the Creator and Saviour Spirit, revealed himself and acted decisively for us in Jesus. I believe in the Divinity of the Holy Ghost, in the sense that the same one God, the Creator and Saviour Spirit, is here and now not far from every one of us; for in him we live and move, in him we have our being, in us, if we consent to know and trust him, he will create the Christlike harvest: love, joy, peace, patience, kindness, goodness, fidelity, gentleness, and self-control" (p. 228).

24. Cf. Paul S. Minear, *Images of the Church in the New Testament* (Westminster Press, 1960). He finds ninety-six images.

25. Cf. Robinson, *The Body;* Best, *One Body in Christ;* E. Schweizer, *The Church as the Body of Christ* (John Knox Press, 1964), and his more extended article on *sōma* in Kittel-Friedrich, Vol. 7.

26. For a "realistic" interpretation, cf. Robinson, *The Body;* for a "metaphorical" interpretation, cf. Best, *One Body in Christ,* and R. H. Gundry, *Sōma in Biblical Theology with Emphasis on Pauline Anthropology* (Cambridge University Press, 1976).

27. Cf. Minear, *Images,* Ch. 6. Cf. Robinson's contrast between "the body of the flesh," "the body of the cross," and "the body of the resurrection" in Paul.

28. Best, *One Body in Christ,* p. 96.

29. Cited in A. Richardson, *An Introduction to the Theology of the New Testament* (New York: Harper & Brothers, 1958; London: SCM, 1958), p. 251.

30. Selby, *Look for the Living,* p. 37.

31. Cf. Rordorf, *Sunday* and Bode, *The First Easter Morning.*

32. C. F. D. Moule, *Worship in the New Testament* (Richmond: John Knox Press, 1961; London: Lutterworth Press, 1961), p. 16.

33. In *Early Christian Fathers,* ed. C. C. Richardson, The Library of Christian Classics (Philadelphia: Westminster Press, 1953; London: SCM, 1953), p. 96.

34. In *The Apostolic Fathers,* Vol. 3, ed. R. A. Kraft (Thomas Nelson & Sons, 1965), p. 130.

35. In Richardson, ed., *Early Christian Fathers,* p. 178.

36. *Ibid.,* p. 287.

37. Cf. note 14 of Chapter 2.

38. Cf. Harald Riesenfeld, "The Gospel Tradition and Its Beginnings," in *The Gospels Reconsidered: A Selection of Papers read at the International Congress on the Four Gospels in 1957* (Oxford: Blackwell, 1960), reprinted in Harald Riesenfeld, *The Gospel Tradition: Essays* (Fortress Press, 1970).

39. M. E. Boring, "The Influence of Christian Prophecy," *New Testament Studies,* Oct. 1978. Cf. also his article, "How May We Identify Oracles of Christian Prophets in the Synoptic Tradition? Mark 3:28–29 as a Test Case," *Journal of Biblical Literature,* Dec. 1972.

40. Boring, "The Influence of Christian Prophecy," pp. 117f.

41. *Ibid.*

42. Cf. Augustin George and others, *Baptism in the New Testament: A Symposium* (Baltimore: Helicon Press, 1964; London: G. Chapman, 1964). Cf. also my *Let Us Worship God* (Richmond: CLC Press, 1966), pp. 100f.

43. Cf. Enoch 12f., in R. H. Charles, *The Apocrypha and Pseudepigrapha of the Old Testament,* Vol. 2 (Oxford: Clarendon Press, 1913), pp. 195ff. Cf. the commentaries on 1 Peter, and Reicke, *The Disobedient Spirits and Christian Baptism* cited above in note 48, Chapter II. Following Rendel Harris' conjecture, Moffatt's translation of the New Testament renders v.19 as: "It was in the Spirit that Enoch also went . . ." He conjectured that *Enōch* was omitted because of its verbal affinity with *en hō kai* in the text. But it is not necessary to alter the text to see the contrast between Enoch and Christ.

44. *The Treatise on the Apostolic Tradition of St. Hippolytus of Rome,* ed. G. Dix (London: SPCK, 1968), p. 34. Cf. also M. E. Boismard, "I Renounce Satan, His Pomps and His Works," in George, *Baptism in the New Testament: A Symposium,* Ch. 5.

45. Bo Reicke, *The Epistles of James, Peter, and Jude,* The Anchor Bible (Doubleday & Co., 1964), p. 111.

46. S. D. Currie, *Koinōnia in Christian Literature to 200 A.D.* (University Microfilms Inc., 1962). He includes a careful study of 1 Corinthians 10–11.

47. The same textual variant (leading to differing translations in RSV and NEB) occurs in the parallel text of Lk. 9:26.

48. Cf. *The Didache* 9 (in Richardson, ed., *Early Christian Fathers,* p. 175):

"Now about the Eucharist: This is how to give thanks: First in connection with the cup:

'We thank you, our Father, for the holy vine of David, your child, which you have revealed through Jesus, your child. To you be glory forever.'

Then in connection with the piece [broken off the loaf]:

'We thank you, our Father, for the life and knowledge which you have revealed through Jesus, your child. To you be glory forever.

'As this piece [of bread] was scattered over the hills and then was brought together and made one, so let your Church be brought together from the ends of the earth into your Kingdom. For yours is the glory and the power through Jesus Christ forever.' . . .

After you have finished your meal, say grace in this way:

'We thank you, holy Father, for your sacred name which you have lodged in our hearts, and for the knowledge and faith and immortality which you have revealed through Jesus, your child. To you be glory forever.' " In this passage there is no reference to the passion. The whole stress is on the new creation.

49. Oscar Cullmann, Ch. 3, in Oscar Cullmann and F. J. Leenhardt, *Essays on the Lord's Supper* (Richmond: John Knox Press, 1958; London: Lutterworth Press, 1958).

50. E.g., *One Baptism, One Eucharist, and a Mutually Recognized Ministry* (Geneva: WCC Faith and Order paper 73, 1975).

51. Neville Clark, *Interpreting the Resurrection* (Philadelphia: Westminster Press, 1967; London: SCM, 1967), pp. 119,120.

52. P. A. van Stempvoort, "The Interpretation of the Ascension in Luke and Acts," in *New Testament Studies,* Oct. 1958.

53. RSV places "and was carried up into heaven" and "worshiped him" in the margin as "non Western interpolations" into the Lukan text. The majority of the members of the committee that edited the third edition of *The Greek New Testament* (United Bible Societies, 1975) disagreed and regarded the longer readings as part of the original text. Cf. Bruce M. Metzger, *A Textual Commentary on the Greek New Testament* (United Bible Societies, 1971), pp. 191–193. So also the 26th ed. of Nestle-Aland (United Bible Societies, 1979).

54. Minear, *Christian Hope and the Second Coming,* pp. 101f.

55. Hans Werner Bartsch, "The Meaning of the Ascension," *The Lutheran Quarterly*, Feb. 1954.

56. Cf. Berkhof, *Christ the Meaning of History*, Ch. 6, "The Crucified Christ in History," and Ch. 7, "The Risen Christ in History."

57. Søren Kierkegaard, *Training in Christianity* (Princeton University Press, 1944), p. 218. Cited in Paul S. Minear, *Horizons of Christian Community* (Bethany Press, 1958), p. 39.

58. Minear, *Horizons of Christian Community*, Ch. 2.

59. Cf. Markus Barth, *The Broken Wall* (Judson Press, 1959); M. Barth and V. Fletcher, *Acquittal by Resurrection*, Part II; Hendrikus Berkhof, *Christ and the Powers* (Herald Press, 1962); A. van den Heuvel, *These Rebellious Powers* (New York: Friendship Press, 1965; London: SCM, 1966).

60. "The Suffering God," in G. A. Studdert-Kennedy, *The Unutterable Beauty, Collected Poetry* (New York and London: Harper & Brothers, n.d.), pp. 2–4.

61. Brown, *The Gospel According to John*, Vol. 2, pp. 778, 771.

62. Paul S. Minear, *To Die and to Live: Christ's Resurrection and Christian Vocation* (Seabury Press, 1977), p. 95.

63. Cited in L. E. Nelson, *Our Roving Bible* (Abingdon-Cokesbury Press, 1945), p. 73.

64. Minear, *To Die and to Live*, p. 98.

65. Cf. Berkhof, *Christ the Meaning of History*, pp. 128ff.

66. Cf. Ladd, *A Commentary on the Revelation of John*, p. 99.

Chapter V. Appropriating the Message of the Resurrection

1. S. D. Currie, "Hope in Its Biblical Settings," in *Austin Seminary Bulletin*, Faculty Edition, April 1969, p. 29.

2. *Ibid.*, p. 30.

3. Moltmann, *Theology of Hope*, p. 20.

4. J. Calvin, *The First Epistle of Paul to the Corinthians* (Grand Rapids: Wm. B. Eerdmans, 1960; Edinburgh: Oliver and Boyd, 1969), p. 283: "Faith and hope are the concomitants of our imperfect state, but love will continue even in the conditions of perfectness."

5. Emil Brunner, *Faith, Hope, and Love* (Philadelphia: Westminster Press, 1956; London: Lutterworth Press, 1957), pp. 13f.

6. *Ibid.*, p. 22.

7. Cf. Moltmann, *Theology of Hope,* pp. 182ff., "The Approach of Form-Criticism to the Easter Narratives and the Questionableness of Its Existentialist Interpretation."

8. From "I Serve a Risen Savior." Words copyright 1964 Renewal Rodeheaver Co., Owner.

9. Karl Barth, *Church Dogmatics* I/2, p. 115.

10. From *The Worshipbook—Services and Hymns* (Westminster Press, 1970), p. 30.

11. Dietrich Bonhoeffer, *Life Together* (Harper & Brothers, 1954), p. 23.

12. Cf. H. Köster on *hypostasis,* in Kittel-Friedrich, Vol. 8, pp. 585ff.

13. Walter Rauschenbusch, *A Theology for the Social Gospel* (Macmillan Co., 1917), p. 235.

14. Brunner, *Faith, Hope, and Love,* p. 51.

15. William Temple, in *The Best of G. A. Studdert-Kennedy* (Harper & Brothers, 1948), p. 6.

16. Thomas à Kempis, *The Imitation of Christ* (Grosset & Dunlap, n.d.), II/24, p. 156. Some of my treatment of John 21 parallels my *Guests of God: Meditations for the Lord's Supper* (Westminster Press, 1956), Ch. 21.

Scripture
Index

Subject and
Author Index